The Other Side

of the River

FROM David Sell
April 2010

The Other Side of the River

When mystical experiences
and strange doctrines
overtake his church,
one man risks all
to find the truth ... a true story

Kevin Reeves

1st Lighthouse Trails Edition
Lighthouse Trails Publishing
Silverton, Oregon

The Other Side of the River
© 2007 by **Kevin Reeves**
First Lighthouse Trails Edition 2007, Second Printing - Fall 2007
Lighthouse Trails Publishing
P.O. Box 958
Silverton, Oregon 97381
www.lighthousetrails.com

Cover photos: "Man on the Beach" ©Aleksey Klementiev; "Misty Golden Morning" ©Lynn Scanzano. Images from BigStockPhoto.com. Other Photos: "Bench in Winter" ©Lanica Klein; "Rangitoto Benched 2" ©Anton Leyland; "Lone Tree at Sunset" ©Dominik Dabrowski. Images from iStockPhoto.com.

Library of Congress Cataloging-in-Publication Data

Reeves, Kevin.
   The other side of the river: when mystical experiences and strange doctrines overtake his church, one man risks all to find the truth : a true story / Kevin Reeves. — 1st Lighthouse Trails ed.
      p. cm.
   Includes bibliographical references and index.
   ISBN 978-0-9791315-0-9 (alk. paper)
   1. Reeves, Kevin. 2. Pentecostals—Biography. 3. Pentecostalism. 4. Theology. I. Title.
   BX8762.Z8R44 2007
   289.9'4092—dc22
   [B]

Other Editions:
iUniverse edition, 2005

Note: Most Lighthouse Trails books are available at special quantity discounts. Contact information for publisher in back of book.

PRINTED IN THE UNITED STATES OF AMERICA

DEDICATION

It is with unspeakable gratitude that I dedicate this book to the glory of God— for His salvation, boundless patience with an erring child, and a Shepherd's love that leads me home.

Unless the LORD had been my help, my soul had almost dwelt in silence. When I said, My foot slippeth; thy mercy, O LORD, held me up. In the multitude of my thoughts within me thy comforts delight my soul. (Psalm 94:17-19)

ACKNOWLEDGEMENTS

This book could not have been written without the love and support of my brothers and sisters across the globe, many of whom I've never met face-to-face. Their patience, love, encouragement, and understanding helped me through some of the toughest times I've ever had. To all of those faithful brothers and sisters—and you know who you are—whose love has helped me to put one tired foot after the other in this walk of truth, from the depths of my heart I want to thank you all.

And special thanks goes to my lovely wife, Kris, without whom my life would be as a wind-blown branch on a cold winter's day. You are my best friend and staunchest ally, whose love for me and for the Gospel has helped more than you know in this contending for the faith.

CONTENTS

Why This Book?

It is my intention that this book will have a two-fold purpose. First, I pray it might be helpful to those who have recognized and turned away from distortions of doctrine and practice that have crept into the church today. Secondly, I hope it will be a warning and an eye-opener to those who are still involved with hyper-charismatic teachings or have loved ones who are. This book is not a diatribe against Pentecostalism. It is a sincere effort to reveal how any group can veer away from biblical Christianity by seeking the mystical and experiential rather than relying on the authority of Scripture.

My own intimate involvement with an aberrational group in no way negates all the good times of fellowship I've had with brothers and sisters whose desire to serve Christ took a dramatic detour from the Scriptures. The church cookouts, parties, and picnics that occurred on a regular basis lent themselves to a joyful expression of community, and the pain of relationships now lost is not a thing lightly endured. The fact that some messages from the pulpit were very good and encouraged biblical holiness makes this kind of public stand even more difficult. A large part of my life was taken up with the people presented herein, and the camaraderie we shared forged a bond broken only with the greatest reluctance and heartache.

This has not been an easy book to write, but the times demand it. I need to make very clear at the outset that the issues presented herein, although intimately personal, are addressed not from any bitterness, but a heartfelt desire to see change. Both in the immediacy of my former congregation and worldwide, the truth must find voice, or many will turn the corner of faith and practice onto the wide avenue of heresy. This is no light thing. Many today have gone the way of Esau and for the sake of a fleeting sensuality are in the process of exchanging their incomparable inheritance in Christ for a bellyful of fleshly experiences.

This book is not an indictment against the heart attitude of pastors who find themselves and their practices mirrored in its pages. Many involved in the "River" movement,* both pastors and congregation members, are sincere, genuine believers who have earnestly desired to serve God and His people. Only God can judge the heart. Every true shepherd wants what is best for the church, and often a seeking church is unwary even when coming face to face with deception. Throughout church history sincere folks have been misled by appearances or good-sounding doctrine. Yet God calls His people back to Himself and promises restoration for those who repent.

The book is a sketch of years spent at my former congregation, including approximately five years as an elder. This is not an exhaustive testament. Should I attempt to catalogue every technique, movement, and ministry we followed and imitated, the resulting volume would be years in the making. The first chapters deal with my *Word of Faith* beginnings and initiation into the popular prophetic arena. The doctrines forming both are a strong part of the source from which the River movement flows. Although there were other tributaries, the Toronto Blessing's *official* origin stems from a message preached by Randy Clark, who received his "impartation" from Rodney Howard-Browne, who himself was holding services in Kenneth Hagin Jr.'s Rhema Bible Church in Tulsa in 1993. Clark's messages in January 1994, at what was then the Toronto Airport Vineyard church, were

---

*The River Movement is an offshoot of the Latter Rain revival, which began in Saskatchewan, Canada in the 1940s. Many other movements sprouted from Latter Rain. Followers believe that the Latter Rain revival is the *latter rain* referred to in such scriptures as Jeremiah 3:3, Joel 2:23, and Hosea 6:3.

the main catalyst for the doctrines, manifestations, and practices we see in the River movement today. In a later chapter we also take the whole issue further back to the "Latter Rain" movement of the late 1940s, which laid the historical groundwork for wide acceptance of "prophetic impartations"* and the experience-based faith seen not only in much of today's Pentecostal and charismatic arenas but also now surfacing in non-charismatic circles as well.

The movement that began at the 1995 Father's Day service at the Brownsville Assembly of God in Pensacola, Florida has also flooded the United States with River doctrine. In spite of protests to the contrary, it is nonetheless the Americanized version of the Toronto Blessing, with nearly all the attendant bizarre manifestations and doctrine. Brownsville leadership long denied any connection with the Canadian outbreak, featuring itself as another sovereign move of God. But anyone who takes the time to study the two movements will see that the Brownsville phenomenon is merely a Toronto clone. Members of the Brownsville church, including Kilpatrick's own wife, traveled to Toronto to experience the "renewal" firsthand.[1] Evangelist Steve Hill, who ministered the "anointing" that Father's Day at Brownsville, received the "blessing" from the leadership of England's Holy Trinity Brompton church, the British implant of the Toronto phenomenon (and the original home of the Alpha course).[2]

Prior to the outbreak of manifestations in Canada in 1994, Toronto pastor John Arnott was also prayed for by long-time friend Benny Hinn.[3] Hinn's doctrines and manifestations, a mixture of Word of Faith theology and his own extra-biblical interpretations, were a precursor to the full-blown "revival." And of course, no background on the River movement is complete without the long-standing practices and doctrines of the Vineyard movement.

While the experiences related in this book are my own, these ministries and many others were strong contributing factors in the way my family and I viewed both God and Christian practice.

---

* Note: Throughout this book, various terms are used that will be in quotation marks when they are first introduced. For the sake of readability, these marks will not be used every time the terms are mentioned.

Since the Alaska ministry with which I was intimately involved was local and had no far-reaching consequences outside our own community, I did not think it necessary to name individuals. With the exceptions of my wife, my eldest daughter, and myself, the names of all local individuals are fictitious; however, the incidents, conversations, and practices discussed are real and accurately depicted. National and international ministers and ministries (like those of Rick Joyner and Kenneth Copeland), which directly affected me and my former group, I have named openly, along with specific references to their works and teachings.

Although not its actual name, New Covenant Fellowship is also real. It still exists, and its leadership, at the time of this writing, is yet intact. The name, New Covenant Fellowship, does not reflect on any other ministry with the same name or any ministry other than the one I had been affiliated with during the time covered in this book. As for the conversations and comments depicted in this book, while the exact wording may at times not be precise, the context in which they are presented and the issues addressed are accurate. I still own a small mountain of sermons on cassette, books from which we learned practice and doctrine, and videos of teachers whose doctrines we circulated. I also own workbooks and other materials that taught us through step-by-step instructions.

To those of my brothers and sisters at New Covenant Fellowship who read this book, please know I love you, and I do not desire in any way to cause pain. I would also exhort any who have become caught in the snare of spiritual deception to return to the Word of God in genuine repentance, for in this alone can there be healing of the grievous wound on the body of Christ.

My heartfelt prayer is that we may once again walk together in the fellowship of the truth.

In Him alone,

Kevin M. Reeves

Spring 2007

Before the Beginning

It was a cool evening for summer, and as the neighborhood was some distance out of town, the area was quiet and dark. The night and solitude worked in our favor, for the gathering itself was not of the barbecue fellowship variety, and I for one wished to avoid unwelcome stares from neighbors. I felt ill at ease in the evening atmosphere of the event. It just didn't feel right, like we were involved in a perversion of something.

About ten of us stood in the backyard of elder Bob Matson's house, knotted together in the gloom and listening intently to instructions. Jason Klein stood as the usual centerpiece. Handing out the bread, which in our case was individual saltine crackers, he reminded us of the importance of our presence there and of the power of what we were about to engage in. He began to pray, and with the bread in our hands, we bowed in agreement with him. I looked around. If others felt fear or nagging doubt, they didn't betray it. Maybe I was the only one out of sorts, just not as spiritual as I should have been. Again.

Putting the crackers to our lips, we ate half, then crumbled the other half and sprinkled it on the ground as we walked in single file around the perimeter of the property. We made a full circle and declared that the body of Christ sanctified the ground. We then did the same with the wine, or in our case grape juice, drinking half and pouring the remainder onto the ground to conform to the property boundaries, thus forming a "blood line." Then came the final prayer:

> Now we give notice to all demons that have inhabited this area that your time is ended. We command you to go now, in the name of Jesus! This property has been claimed for the kingdom of God, so go!

Amid all the smiles and rejoicing, I had a sick feeling in the pit of my stomach. I was glad to just go home.

Learned from Gwen Shaw's book *Redeeming the Land*,[1] this practice was utilized in our church for "breaking the curse of the enemy" upon our town, as we liked to put it. This was one of a host of methods for removing the stranglehold of sin and religious stodginess over both the people and the land. As matriarch of End Time Handmaidens, a prophetic group composed mostly of women who minister throughout the world via publications and in person, Gwen Shaw spoke with authority. I met her once, when she was invited to speak at our congregation of New Covenant Fellowship, in the late 1980s, and I have to admit being impressed with her angelic face and what I then perceived to be a godly demeanor. An attractive woman probably in her fifties at the time, she spoke humbly, and as we sang some of the old hymns I love that were never a part of our group's corporate worship, she won me over without a struggle. Attended by another older woman whose name I've long forgotten, Mrs. Shaw's sermon focused on the doctrinal abuses within the Catholic Church, spotlighting the specific practices of certain penitent of the Roman clergy. Priests would abuse their bodies to the point of death with self-imposed penance in order to secure acceptance into heaven. Having spent twenty-four loyal years within the ranks of Roman Catholicism, even memorizing the Mass in Latin, I was understandably horrified. Yet I well knew that such abuses were indeed possible. The Catholic Church's emphasis of salvation through an unceasing battery of good works was a fertile breeding ground for fanaticism.

So I was quite taken with Gwen Shaw. Were we purposely duped? I suppose it depends on your definition of the word purposely. The sincerity with which she presented her case seemed genuine. And the books she brought with her for sale (and there were lots of them) seemed to speak powerfully to the need of our community. We were a *cutting-edge* church, and these were the tools to get the job done. In the back of one of her books, an advertisement showcased a supposed recording of the angelic host singing along with a choir—I was wowed and wanted to hear it. In *Redeeming the Land*, when Mrs. Shaw outlined a host of demonic entities, their specific abilities, and their assignments over geographic locations, I was enthralled. In that same book, she presented the testimony of one man who said he had died and was taken by the angel of the Lord to view and record all the demonic principalities and powers so that the church might more successfully prevail against them.[2] Hearing this, I craved more.

Although she obviously believed them, the very practices and teachings outlined in some of these volumes presented tremendous obstacles to a Bible-believing Christian. And the group's extreme preoccupation with angelic beings led to extra-biblical beliefs and manifestations, some of which are documented in the book *Our Ministering Angels*.[3] This compilation of anecdotes and supposition mixed with a certain amount of Scripture merge doctrine and personal experience to convince the reader that people resemble their assigned "guardian angel,"[4] that the "photograph" of angels over a coffin is genuine,[5] that angels are seen in the most unusual places, such as a car hood,[6] and that an angel joined in worship at the community of Engeltal.[7] Mrs. Shaw claims she has had many interactions with angels. She writes that once while walking in Jerusalem's Garden Tomb area, she heard the spiritual hosts singing the resurrection hymn sung by them on the morning of our Lord's rising from the dead.[8] Of course, she acknowledges that precedent for this cannot be found in Scripture, but she heard it nevertheless, and the reader is left with the impression that to argue with her is to deny spiritual reality. Hers seemed to be the voice of authority.

Her strange doctrines found willing ears and hungry hearts in my former congregation.

What needs to be understood is that most, if not all of us at New Covenant Fellowship, were truly desirous of serving the Lord and fighting the good fight of faith. Like so many other independent charismatic churches, we wanted to see souls saved and the miraculous power of God manifest in healings, deliverances, and the gifts of the Holy Spirit. But there was an underlying factor, a premise woven throughout the fabric of our church probably from its inception—elitism. We were the fortunate ones, called to walk in the authority that the church was so bereft of in these last days.

Through its own incompetence and adherence to legalism and dead religious doctrines, we were repeatedly told, the body of Christ had surrendered the wisdom and power that came from knowing Him. It was up to us at New Covenant to demonstrate that God's kingdom power was real and available to every Christian in our town. This prideful mindset was a recipe for disaster. Our heartfelt desire to belong, a need to submit to spiritual authority, and the hidden agenda of the flesh to be one of the super-anointed took their toll on our church's scriptural integrity.

My former congregation was not alone in its beliefs then, nor are they now. All across the world, many groups like this are given over to the excitement of carnal manifestations, esoteric wisdom, and elitist mentality. In fact, this thinking within the charismatic community has grown so common as to minimize the legitimacy of those who simply want to serve Jesus and know the Word of God. Anymore, that's old hat. The "new thing" demands subservience to the experiential, and the current trend of gross subjectivism doesn't allow for old fashioned adherence to Scripture as the basis of faith and practice.

These are critical days for the body of Christ. We are in the epoch of church history spoken of by the apostle Paul as "perilous times" (II Timothy 3:1). What makes the danger all the more imminent is that not much of the church believes it. Many of us have owned the glorious but erroneous vision of an end-times remnant walking in unconquerable power, transforming entire societies. The result has been nothing short of catastrophic. How soon we forget. Every cult in the world has sprouted from the fertile soil of deception, always initiated by a drastic move away from the *primacy* of the Word of God into the nebulous, self-defining atmosphere of experience. At New Covenant, our desire to accumulate otherworldly wealth (i.e., supernatural power) had ushered us into a contrived system of personal spiritual elevation much like such active cults as Mormonism and the Jehovah's Witnesses.

In the case of my former congregation, our pre-supposed love of the Word of God, along with our ignorance of and opposition to nearly every scriptural warning about false doctrine and seducing spirits in the church, left us open to bizarre teachings and practices. As we embraced mysticism, our biblical parameters melted away. Yes, we were sincere, but what we were wanting was diametrically opposed to our relationship with Jesus Christ.

Like physical signs of pain, there were signs in our church that something was terribly wrong. But just like the person who ignores the pain and avoids going to the doctor, we too ignored what should have been so obvious. That is, until it got so bad that avoidance was no longer an option.

Why do people ignore warning signs? It's like a motorist painting over his oil pressure gauge so he won't notice the depleting measure. But the reality of the situation will become evident enough when his engine seizes up, and the car comes to a sudden halt. I've discovered that in the spiritual arena most people will do exactly this: they take pains to look the other way when something bumps up against their doctrine. As a Christian, there's no quicker way to start a fight with a friend than to tell him that some of his most fervent beliefs are wrong. I know. I've lost my share of friendships that way. The problem comes when folks aren't willing to deal with the uncomfortable. And the horror of it is that in spiritual matters, we're dealing with eternal things. While the person who ruins his vehicle can at least purchase another, the human soul is irreplaceable.

What we believe and place our trust in will certainly determine our eternal destiny, regardless of our sincerity. The Mormon missionaries who have come to my house have seemed to be some of the most sincere people I've ever known, but they are hopelessly lost, believing a perverse doctrine that, unless repented of, will surely deliver them to an everlasting hell. Their beliefs will turn them onto a distinctly hazardous route called the broad way (Matthew 7:13). As tightly as they cling to the hope of exaltation to godhood, it will not prevent them from slipping into a godless eternity. Their experience with *God*, exemplified by the "burning in the bosom," has them so convinced that no matter what, they will not entertain doctrine that conflicts with their belief system. Part of it is fear, promulgated by "apostles and prophets," whom they believe to be a living link to God Himself. They are firmly entrenched in the idea that, should they consider Joseph Smith to have been a false prophet, they are forever doomed.

In my own case, association with a cutting-edge group offered me security and personal power, and for years, the paranoia of offending God kept me from asking too many unsettling questions. It's ironic that, in a fellowship that taught a watered-down version of the fear of the Lord, it was fear that motivated me to stay put.

Many other Christians find themselves in this same predicament, especially those with a genuine heart for the truth. When some doctrine foreign to biblical Christianity is introduced into the congregation, they want to inquire about its origin and validity, but fear holds them in check. If it comes from the pastor, who surely must be more spiritual than the rest of the group, then God must simply have approved it. Therefore, questioning or opposing the pastor or church leadership is seen as opposing the Lord Himself.

But God doesn't work that way. Throughout the Bible are examples of those who love the Lord who questioned authority when it was wrong. And what's more, "prove all things" is clearly God's instruction to the believer (1 Thessalonians 5:21).

Those Who Resist

This manipulative pastoral attitude of squelching sincere inquiries was recently brought home in a frightening way. A friend of mine attended a local church service, knowing that the pastor was fully in support of the so-called Brownsville revival. She was nonetheless unprepared for the chilling threat from the pulpit. After reminding the congregation of the judgment deaths of Ananias and Sapphira for opposing the Holy Spirit, the pastor looked directly at the congregation and said, "If you think about questioning anything that goes on in this service … well, you just be careful!"

Two plus two still equals four. His meaning was quite plain. If you want to end up like that evil-hearted couple, just go ahead and do some serious inquiry into the teachings or manifestations of this group.

Brothers and sisters, something is seriously wrong here. Brutalizing the saints with a threat from an angry heart is not the Bible way. But it is becoming quite a fashionable pastime for leadership to silence even well-intentioned criticism with threats and ridicule. It has been going on from both the Toronto and Brownsville pulpits for years and has spilled over into many other groups in the church today. Name calling and ostracizing are common methods to silence critics. Names like hypocrites, Sanhedrin, and God mockers are merely a sampling of the invective aimed at Christians who are concerned about doctrinal error. Nobody wants to be labeled a Pharisee or heresy hunter. But that is often the penalty for daring to step out and ask for a public, biblical accounting of doctrine and practice.

I know the feeling first hand. I have more than once been called legalistic and have been accused of "going down a hard path"—one of my own making, of course. I had been told repeatedly that I was spiritually immature and had not understood the importance of such works as Rick Joyner's *The Final Quest* [9]—despite its un-biblical concepts and many outright contradictions to Scripture.

A current *river* is flowing, which many believe to be of God. Removed from its proper setting in the 47th chapter of Ezekiel, which speaks of a stream gushing out from the Temple of God, this passage in Scripture is today used to promote a last days vision for the church. In its proper context in Ezekiel, this wonderful prophecy is an encouragement that God has not forgotten His covenant people of Israel. But overstepping the sanctity of scriptural boundaries, this passage has been reshaped into the comfortable doctrines of the easy believism and sensual manifestations that mark a massive shift in the church. As believers, we have taken a hairpin turn from the preeminence of the Word of God to a relative, experiential, and terribly apostate faith.

The River Revival movement—encompassing the Toronto Blessing, Brownsville Revival (or Pensacola Outpouring), Dominion, Latter Rain, Word of Faith, Rodney Howard-Browne's laughing revival, the Kansas City prophets, and an arbitrary mix of all or some of the aforementioned—is flowing into congregations worldwide. Given impetus by these major doctrinal tributaries, this movement's teachings have led multitudes away from the truths of the Gospel of Jesus Christ into a dangerous realm of subjective experiences, mysticism, and blatant heresy. Closely follow the curves of this *river* and you'll find spiritual deviations at first overlooked. After all the hype, the wild manifestations, the wonderful testimonies, the flamboyant prophecies, and the earth-shaking visions, the discerning eye will gaze upon a farther shore, where an entirely different, frightening story unfolds—a story of broken lives and shattered faith, of rebellion and of merchandising a substitute "anointing."

There is another side to all the fanfare, a glaring *something* that for the most part remains unspoken or deliberately avoided. There is indeed another side to the *River*. The story you are about to read is my personal journey in finding it. As believers, it is time we cross over and take a long, hard look.

CHAPTER 1

THE EMERGENCE OF THE God-MEN

"In you dwells all the fullness of the Godhead in bodily form."

Jason preached from Colossians 2:9 with his usual pacing, his face intense as he drove home the point. The problem was, he was not referring to Christ, "in you dwells all the fullness" but was instead referring to us, the congregation. For me, it was a new teaching, one I had never heard before. I didn't know whether to be awed or scared. This corruption of the Colossians verse was to be the basis of much of what we sought to accomplish at New Covenant Fellowship.

We had to be built up, Jason said, and the way to do that was to really *know* who we were in Christ. The power, the authority, the life from heaven flowed from the throne of Almighty God to His own elect, and if we only realized the explosive potential resident within us, we would walk with ease in the supernatural realm. Miracles would be common, diseases would flee at a touch from our hands, and demons would hightail it to the nearest exit when we walked into a room. We could bind, loose, command angels and even order the elements around. This was only a smattering of what was proclaimed from the front of our meeting room on Sunday mornings and at mid-week meetings.

The lure of godhood for man is the oldest bait in the annals of history, dating from the serpent's temptation to Eve in the Garden of Eden. The question "Yea, hath God said…" (Genesis 3:1) precipitated the greatest tragedy of the human race. And man has been trying to get back to the Garden ever since. Even the church has not been immune to this desire. Sad to say, in 1988 neither was I. Suffering from the echoes of a season of backsliding, I wanted desperately to be led into a deeper walk with Christ—cemented in relationship to Him. I had the Word and the Holy Spirit to guide me, of course, but I was afraid that they alone weren't enough. I was ripe for accompanying *signs and wonders* to validate my calling. That's when I met Jason.

Master and Disciple

From our first encounter, I recognized that Jason Klein spoke with an authority, a charisma that drew people to him, particularly those of us who came from mainstream Christianity. Discontent had forged a common bond, for the core group had come from other area churches and clustered around Jason like cells to a healing wound. He had been sent from a large city to plant a church in our town, and although only a handful originally welcomed him in that endeavor, within two years the congregation grew to about seventy-five people. It was about that time, in the summer of 1988 that my wife Kris and I arrived.

Jason seemed to sincerely love people, and his giving heart sought out those in need. He was a toucher, lavishing congregants with hugs and handshakes, and always hunting an opportunity to fellowship closely with the people of God. But a thoughtful backward glance confirms other, disturbing characteristics that should have sent up red flags in my mind. He had a habit of getting uncomfortably close when speaking with a person, crowding the other's space. With his face only inches away and his eyes intense while he spoke, a subtle manipulation (perhaps unconsciously) herded you into a predetermined direction. As a hugger, he would embrace nearly anyone, at times to the recipient's discomfort. And there was never any real question regarding his authority in spiritual matters. He was always deferred to, for he seemed to *know*, even if his stance was skewed in relation to Scripture.

In conversations, he assured me that God was not to be feared, only loved and respected, something he reiterated endlessly from the pulpit. As God's children of the New Testament, the old "fear of the

Lord" was something pretty much of the past—non-applicable to the believer in Jesus. Disturbed because I'd read exactly the opposite in Luke 12:4-5, I once gently disagreed with him. Of course, I was immediately corrected, him proving me wrong with his irresistible authority; although I gave in, I was not fully convinced. The incident would prove to be one of many that I would file away for further analysis when the tide had turned.

Jason was the hub of the wheel, and so I guess that made us the spokes. We radiated out from him and his words, and we felt cohesiveness in him. His unchallenged strength was further abetted when he took someone under his wing, teaching what he believed were the deeper things of God, and helping the believer get established in other areas of his life.

I now believe Jason was a hurting man. His deep need for acceptance played out in his unrelenting judgment of the *legalistic* portion of the body of Christ, in his comforting of those in emotional or physical pain, his expansive generosity, and his need to control. There were areas outside the realm of New Covenant Fellowship where he did help Kris and me. He occasionally provided me with much-needed work, and allowed me to house-sit a couple of weeks in his spacious home during the time our young family lived in a freezing, sardine-sized travel trailer. He also took up several collections for us to purchase a vehicle when we owned none. I must honestly say that I grew to love the man; a part of me still does.

Unorthodox Introduction

Kris and I first met Jason in the summer of 1988. We came to the small idyllic town that spring on a second honeymoon and were taken with the beauty and wildness of the area. After praying about it, we decided the Lord was leading us there. Belonging at that time to a wonderful, biblically-solid group of people, we felt sad to move from our moorings, but knew it was time to go. With our little redhead Megan, we packed up what few belongings we could tote, and with a mixture of sadness and anticipation, we headed north.

From day one, there were problems. It was the height of the tourist season, and some of the townsfolk saw us as outsiders and made us feel most unwelcome. A lot of people came to town in order to work summers and then flee south come cold weather—in other words, they socked away money garnered from a struggling community and then left with it. Folks didn't know we intended to remain; therefore, work was hard to come by, as was a place to stay. We finally settled on a tiny 12x15 trailer at the edge of a youth hostel, where I could work off the meager $200 monthly rent.

I visited some of the main churches in town and just wasn't satisfied. I wanted a church that offered a Pentecostal-style atmosphere—that's when I stumbled across New Covenant Fellowship. Although there was a certain feel about the place that didn't sit exactly right with me, the worship seemed good, the gifts of the Spirit appeared to be in operation, and importantly, I was welcomed warmly. I brought Kris with me my next time around.

It was an interesting first service as a family. Our little squirmer Megan, not quite a year-and-a-half old, didn't take too kindly to the two-hour meeting. While standing in the back of the rented building, Kris and I quietly argued about who would take the baby home. In the midst of my attempts to lift Megan out of Kris's arms, we heard loudly from the pulpit, "Could you folks come up here, please? You have a word from the Lord."

We froze rather ridiculously, child in midair, arguments falling silently to the carpeted floor, faces no doubt grimacing in embarrassment as every eye in the place fell on us. We had no choice but to parade up to the front where Jason stood smiling, flanked by his two elders Bob Matson and Tom Smalley. They laid hands on us, and we received our first taste of "personal prophecy."*

Jason spoke for the Lord: "Don't be afraid, for I have called you to this place. I have seen your needs and will supply them all." I noticed that Jason didn't speak to me but to Kris, leaning close as she held Megan and saying things that a frightened woman in a rocky marriage

---

* Note: Throughout this book, various terms are used that will be in quotation marks when they are first introduced. For the sake of readability, these marks will not be used every time the term is mentioned.

in a strange place wanted to hear. Nevertheless, from that time the die was cast. We were officially received into the group, and I guess at the time we were relieved to finally have somewhere to belong.

The Copeland Connection

Although he worked it to the hilt, Jason cannot be faulted for the origination of this god/man heresy. He picked it up quite naturally from the Word of Faith works of Kenneth Copeland and his older mentor, Kenneth ("Dad") Hagin, both of whom have taught for decades that the believer in Christ is literally a god on earth. Word of Faith's doctrines—of Christ's taking the nature of Satan on the Cross, His supposed rebirth in hell (the first born-again man!), and the completed atonement purchased not by the blood of the Cross but Jesus' paying for our sins in anguished torment in hell—were things hidden from us during our stay at New Covenant Fellowship.[1] Had we been aware of these heresies, we both would have likely made an unceremonious exit.

Many years have now passed since the original proclamation of these doctrines by Hagin, Copeland, and company, but the men (and women) who have made these statements and many others like them have not repented. These teachings have been an intricate part of the whole pattern of false doctrine in these people's ministries. In their eyes, Jesus becomes merely the "pattern Son"[2] who, although lip service is given to His uniqueness, beckons us to follow and through Him take up our own mantle of godhood.

Known as Word of Faith, Word-Faith, the Faith movement, Health and Wealth, the Prosperity Gospel, or sometimes Positive Confession, the basic doctrine is a hodgepodge of the fraudulent mixed in with enough truth to give it a scriptural veneer. To the initiate, which we all were at that time with the exception of Jason himself, Word of Faith's basic doctrine hails from the idea that faith is an impersonal "force" that can be wielded by the believer (and even pagans) for personal benefit. If the Christian will simply believe, and speak aloud his desire, the result is guaranteed. A big part of this formula system is based upon a tremendous twisting of the words of Jesus, recorded in Mark 11:23:

> For verily I say unto you, That whosoever shall say unto
> this mountain, Be thou removed, and be thou cast into the
> sea; and shall not doubt in his heart, but shall believe that
> those things which he saith shall come to pass; he shall have
> whatsoever he saith.

Now, every true believer knows in his heart that we simply cannot ask for anything we want and have it granted, regardless of the will of God. This is easily established by a reading of I John 5:14-15:

> And this is the confidence that we have in him, that, if we
> ask any thing according to his will, he heareth us: And if we
> know that he hear us, whatsoever we ask, we know that we
> have the petitions that we desired of him.

Scripture is replete with examples of men asking, and receiving only when it is in accordance with God's own wishes, not ours. To deny this is to deny the very sovereignty of the Lord and His only written record:

> Ye lust, and have not: ye kill, and desire to have, and cannot
> obtain: ye fight and war, yet ye have not, because ye ask not.
> Ye ask, and receive not, because ye ask amiss, that ye may
> consume it upon your lusts. (James 4:2-3)

But Word of Faith doctrine sidesteps the issue because its adherents are taught that the world belongs not to God, but to men. It is to men, they say, whom God has given *dominion* (remember that word), and to men that He has given authority to exercise on matters spiritual and temporal. As the reasoning goes, God's promises in His Word speak generously of material blessings upon His faithful, and, as God is a man of His word, if I remain faithful to Him, I can ask anything in the name of Jesus, and it will be done for me. Didn't Christ Himself say that very thing in John 14:13-14?

The main issue here is power. The Health and Wealth doctrine did not earn that name by default. I've never seen a television evangelist (at least, not the ones regularly featured on the Trinity Broadcasting Network) wearing inexpensive shoes, suits, and watches. "Only the best for kids of the King," is the monotonous refrain from people in the Word of Faith camp. Such beliefs are considered only the very basics in their form of spiritual instruction.

Power, Power, Who's Got the Power?

These soulish cravings for power are hard to resist, even for the committed, knowledgeable Christian. By knowledgeable, I mean understanding and following the doctrine given in Scripture. Many believers love the Lord but attempt to follow Him in a way diametrically opposed to the way He reveals Himself in His Word. Biblical ignorance is fertile ground for the tiniest seed of heresy.

This was our biggest problem. At the time of our introduction into New Covenant Fellowship, Kris had been saved only briefly. I had accepted Christ a year-and-a-half earlier than she had, but a year of that had been spent in horrible backsliding. I felt constantly inferior and condemned because of my sin during that time, although I had repented. Word of Faith, along with its theological compatriots Dominion/Kingdom Now, stroked my battered personality. If God granted me power, I reasoned, then surely I must be forgiven.

Manifestations of the spiritual realm were the big issue; it was universally believed that these took place only under the *anointing,* and whoever happened to be the catalyst at the time was being greatly blessed and recognized by God. And while true humility would compel one to bow in adoration of God, a two-fisted grasping for power was actually the end result. I well recall when, having been "delivered" of a variety of demons, for the longest time afterward I went around shouting angrily at every "demon" in existence (and a good many which don't exist), pleased at the authority of exorcism residing in me.

Some of the preaching concerning the grace of Christ helped me to be rid of the condemnation, but only as long as it was within scriptural bounds. That much did some good, and I believe it was preached out of love for the Lord and His people. Christ came the first time not to judge the world, but to save the world (John 3:17), and I needed to be reminded that I was indeed forgiven. The major glitch came when we transposed grace into power, not power to live a holy life, but power to walk in the miraculous and what we viewed as the supernatural. While we are certainly given authority by Jesus, we in no way can match Him or become His earthly substitute. We were erroneously taught that in us "all the fullness of Deity dwells in bodily form," and the result was predictable.

For instance, sickness was always considered an attack of the devil, and demons and their works were regularly cursed when the victims of ailments were prayed for. Not infrequently, a demon was commanded to leave the body of the sufferer. This was standard form, for demon inhabitation of Christians was considered the norm. As we believed this, exorcism among our membership was routine. However, the term exorcism had been replaced by the more palatable term deliverance, but given the concept of demonic inhabitation and the need to cast it out, the practice was really the same.

The Curse of Childbirth

As disciples with authority, we were tutored that we were redeemed from the curse of original sin, and all it entailed. As pain in childbirth was considered a part of the curse, and since we were redeemed, our wives should experience comfortable delivery. Jason told that very thing to Kris, and when our second child was born after a healthy set of painful uterine contractions, Kris felt that she had failed God. Her little faith, she reasoned, had shamed her Lord.

What a tragedy—to lay a burden of guilt upon a woman doing her level best to follow Christ, and leave her devastated with a manufactured failure! And for what? Experiencing pain in childbirth, of all things! Jesus refuted this heresy two millennia ago:

> A woman when she is in travail hath sorrow, because her hour is come: but as soon as she is delivered of the child, she remembereth no more the anguish, for joy that a man is born into the world. (John 16:21)

If Jesus considered childbearing pain a normal part of life, then who are we to argue?

That's not to say that Jason would have been unsympathetic to her pain. But he wouldn't have refuted his anti-curse stance either. While consoling those who didn't live up to the tenets of this "beyond the curse" doctrine, he nonetheless reaffirmed his unmoving position on it, counseling us to continue to strive to "just believe God." The thing is, it wasn't God in whom we had placed our faith. To a large extent it was Jason, whom we absolutely looked upon as the Lord's anointed. So we continued to strive, to bring our thoughts *into line* with what we believed to be thoughts of God, and to take dominion in His authority.

Whose World Is It Anyway?

This "dominionist" mentality also prodded us into some bizarre antics. One Sunday morning at church, Jason spoke about the poor year plaguing the local commercial fishermen and the financial hardship it had brought upon the community. Striding back and forth in the front of the building, he loudly declared, "In the name of Jesus, I command fish to come into the nets of the fishermen, so full that they are overflowing."

He continued in this vein for some time, "taking authority" over the sea life a stone's throw from our rented meeting house in order to have salmon and halibut hauled into boats by our fisher folk. He reasoned that if Jesus did it (Luke 5:4-9), then so could we. For me, this logic translated into the personal realm, and I know I didn't act alone. With shame, I have to admit I tried this same tactic many times when I went sport fishing, commanding the fish to come to my hook.

By the way—it didn't work. Surprise, huh? What I discovered was that asking in humility resulted in a much better track record of answered prayer.

In June of 1997, then-pastor Tom Smalley echoed Jason's belief. He stated in a sermon that as believers in Christ, we have been given dominion over the world, including the elements themselves. With zeal, Tom noted that God is calling His church to take back the do-minion we have given to Satan. When Jesus rebuked the storm and changed the weather, Tom said He was merely revealing to us the power God has breathed into us to do the same thing.

Now, that provokes a question—if Adam was granted dominion in the Garden of Eden (Genesis 1:28), why didn't he exercise power over the sky, wind, etc? In fact, the apostles never held this kind of doctrine, and they were responsible for setting out in orderly form the teachings revealed by the Spirit of God. What we engage in as Christians must be rooted in apostolic practice. If the apostles who knew our Lord—who ate with Him, touched Him, and were witnesses to His resurrection—had no concept of the ideas being promoted today, then we flirt with these power trips to our own disaster.

Certainly some amazing miracles involving the weather did indeed occur in Scripture (Joshua 10:12-13, I Kings 17:1, 18:41-45), but God was petitioned in prayer for those events to take place. Plus, contrary to what believers are now told to expect in their daily lives, these recorded instances were not the norm, but the extraordinary. All three incidents referenced here apparently happened only once for Joshua and Elijah. Peter did walk on the sea with Jesus, but again, it is through Christ's power and not something "imparted" to Peter that these things took place. Yes, Peter walked on water, but only once. Yes, he walked on the waves, but only at the invitation of the Son of God. Had he stepped out of the boat with a dominion mindset, he would have quickly discovered his buoyancy quotient and crawled back into the ship dripping wet and perhaps a bit wiser.

From the Sunday pulpit also came a statement that I recognized immediately as counter-scriptural. This teaching still resounds today throughout many hyper-charismatic groups, that believers can actually call things into existence, to essentially create with a god-like power.

"We call those things which be not as though they were" (paraphrased from KJV). This incredible corruption of Romans 4:17 removes creative authority from its rightful place—with *God alone*. Scripture does not give Christians carte blanche in the supernatural realm. Although the glory for this power in us was ostensibly given to God, the doctrine derived its existence from the twisting of Colossians 2:9. The fact is we cannot create anything, and no amount of wishing or positive confession will alter that fact. Although I kept my opinions to myself on this one, I never did add it to my statement of faith.

The basis of all this is the incredibly strange Word of Faith belief that even God, speaking on the first day of creation, had faith in His words to form worlds. Did you hear that? God had to have faith in order to create! Therefore, our faith could do the same thing, since He lives within us. It is standard Word of Faith doctrine that faith is a "force," and anyone who knows the tricks can tap into this force and operate it to his own gain. Although this teaching is absent from the Bible, it *is* found within the writings of Mary Baker Eddy of Christian Science fame. This metaphysical cult has always taught the creative power of both the mind and positive confession.

Word of Faith also claimed that since Adam had been given dominion of the entire world in the Garden, when he fell that same authority had passed to Satan. God was then a helpless outsider who needed to scheme to regain from the hosts of hell what He had lost. The Messiah was God's answer to the problem. When Christ came, these teachers say, He restored all dominion to His elect; thus we may claim the very authority of the Godhead in commanding the elements of nature into our desired order, and speak our desires into existence.

We need to get one thing straight. Contrary to Word of Faith theology, God never lost control of this world. He never was "on the outside looking in," as some proponents have put it. The Almighty God created everything in existence, has always had complete ownership, and always had all authority to do with it just as it pleased Him:

> The earth is the LORD's, and the fulness thereof; the world, and they that dwell therein. (Psalm 24:1)

> For every beast of the forest is mine, and the cattle upon a thousand hills. I know all the fowls of the mountains: and the wild beasts of the field are mine. If I were hungry, I would not tell thee: for the world is mine, and the fulness thereof. (Psalm 50:10-12)

Mine hand also hath laid the foundation of the earth, and my right hand hath spanned the heavens: when I call unto them, they stand up together. (Isaiah 48:13)

Doesn't sound too much like the impotent god of Word of Faith teaching. And that is exactly the point. Word of Faith denigrates the power and uniqueness of the one true God and at the same time elevates man to the status of godhood. This kind of religious persuasion is straight from the pages of the book of Mormon, with one minor exception. While Mormon doctrine promises LDS believers a *future* rulership of their own world, attainable only after death and subsequent exaltation, Word of Faith Christians get to do it here and now. That is, if you buy into this heresy.

Just How Positive Is It?

As Word of Faith adherents, we were taught never to confess the negative, only what we viewed as encouraging. "Positive Confession" was key to realizing kingdom benefits. If we had physical pain, we proclaimed, "[B]y whose stripes ye were healed." (I Peter 2:24). If in financial difficulty, we'd wield the confession, "Thank you, God, that You 'rebuke the devourer' for my sake because I tithe" (from Malachi 3:11). It is amazing how the "devourer" was always equated with some demonic entity trying to consume our finances! And, I recall one occasion that I still have to shake my head over, even though at the time it had me thinking: I once owned a red flannel shirt that I really liked. It was quite threadbare, but it was comfortable, fit well, and had a warmth of familiarity about it that just kind of sat well with me. Then-elder Tom Smalley happened to come to our house one day, and seeing me in this shirt declared in all seriousness, "You know, that shirt is a confession of poverty." At first, I smiled and disregarded his words, but after he left the house, I began to mull it over. Was my choice of clothing actually inhibiting the flow of finances from the throne of God? It began to bother me. I certainly didn't want to be guilty of robbing my family of financial blessing. This sounds funny in hindsight, but it gives a vivid illustration of the bondage this kind of thinking brings on. If I

had to surrender my preferred attire, what would be the next target—
hobbies or my free time? Would I now have to choose between the
things I enjoyed doing and what might be considered activities more
appropriate to an inheritor of financial wealth?

You see, on and on it goes. It never really stops. Something as
simple as a shirt became an obstacle to the freedom I should have
been enjoying in Christ.

Now certainly we should not live sloppily and let vile things pour
out of our mouths, but there is a major difference between simple,
holy living, and being controlled by an outside entity (Positive Confession). One brings liberty, the other manipulation. I wonder what
the apostles would say about all this, or how the Positive Confession
group would receive them. According to some in the Word of Faith
higher echelon (e.g., John Avanzini), Jesus wore rich clothing and
carried around a moneybag with our present-day equivalent of tens
of thousands of dollars.[3] Would the apostles, who were considered
scum by the world (I Corinthians 4:9-13), be welcome in Word of
Faith/Positive Confession conferences? I doubt it, at least not without
a shave, a bath, and appropriate designer apparel.

Sickness Be Gone!

Dominion/Kingdom Now/Word of Faith also has a lot to say about
healing. I understand the Scriptures in relation to prayer and healing for our physical bodies, but that is not what we are dealing with
in these heretical theologies, which teach that the believer in Christ
should not only be healed of sickness, but walk in complete "divine
health." In other words, we don't ever have to get sick. The reasoning
behind this is a twisting of the scripture in II Peter 1:4, where the
apostle states, "[Y]e might be partakers of the divine nature."

In actuality, this particular reference has to do with our inheritance in
Christ and being grafted into the true vine, which is Jesus (John 15:4-5).
This has nothing to do with the supposed revelation that we are somehow divine and should not suffer the consequences of living in a fallen
world. This false teaching is not new at all, but it was given greater
voice in the 20th century church than ever before, and no doubt its

influence will continue to grow in the 21st century church. Some of the leading promoters of the Faith movement have stated that God and man were on equal terms in the Garden. Progressive reasoning dictates that if it was so before the curse, so it must now be with Christians, who have been redeemed from the curse of the law.

Equality with God? We need to think this one through. If Hagin and Copeland are serious, then no real distinction between Christ and us exists. And that is exactly the point of becoming a god on earth. The teaching has us literally becoming an incarnation, like Jesus. The upshot of this belief system is that if we are Christ, as Hagin has also stated, and have our own incarnation, then we should have all the attending benefits of that state of being, including perpetual freedom from sickness.

Can I tell you that in my many years in this movement, I have never once known *anyone* who did not suffer from a common cold, the flu, aches, pains, or infirmity? You won't hear this fact spread abroad, but the Word of Faith camp has just as much sickness, disease, and death as the staunchest fundamentalists.

In his revealing article, "Death by Faith," missionary Mike Oppenheimer of Let Us Reason ministries catalogues the embarrassing frequency of sickness and death in the Word of Faith camp and its associates.[4] E.W. Kenyon, one of the principal early expositors of Word of Faith theology, died of a malignant tumor. Joyce Meyer underwent medical treatment for breast cancer. Kenneth Hagin's sister and brother-in-law both died of cancer. John Osteen died after a battle with kidney and heart diseases. Kathryn Kuhlman died of heart failure. Jamie Buckingham, frequent contributor to *Charisma* magazine, died of cancer after repeatedly claiming himself healed. John Wimber of Vineyard fame died of complications due to his battle with cancer. "Prophetess" Ruth Ward Heflin, whose appearance on the international charismatic scene was heralded by the appearance of "gold dust" falling on her audiences, recently died of cancer. Faith healers Jack Coe, who died of bulbar polio, and A. A. Allen, whose official cause of death was cited as cardiac arrest, are often portrayed as pillars of charismatic Christendom. Oral Roberts, who has perhaps laid hands on more people for healing than anyone in the last thirty years, experienced chest pains and was admitted to a hospital suffering from a heart attack that nearly proved fatal. At least Roberts doesn't forbid medical attention for his followers. In fact, the university named for him houses a medical school.

And now, Kenneth Hagin, Sr. himself died in September 2003, after several days in a cardiac intensive care unit.

The examples are manifold, but these few suffice. The very leaders of the divine health movement have had to resort to doctors in order to preserve their lives. For us, that should be clue #2, following hard on the heels of clue #1, which is the heretical nature of their doctrine in light of the Word of God. Those interested in an in-depth examination of the Word of Faith camp should check out D. R. McConnell's *A Different Gospel.*[5] After more than twenty-five years, it is still the standard reference work on the subject, and rightly so. McConnell's piercing analysis exposes the falsehoods and scriptural gymnastics upon which the movement's doctrines are built.

The most oft-quoted text for healing is I Peter 2:24. If we knew nothing else at New Covenant Fellowship about our sickness being removed from us, we needed to have this verse as part of our claim on divine health—"by whose stripes ye were healed" became the catch phrase to deal with everything from headaches to cancer. Popularized by E.W. Kenyon in the early part of this century and utilized by Hagin, Copeland, and most of the leaders of the Word of Faith camp, this text got its strength from the supposed revelation that Christ's atonement removed not only sin but sickness from the believer forever. It is only up to us to claim the promise as divine right.

But a closer look at the full context of the verse shines a very different light on the subject:

> Who his own self bare our sins in his own body on the tree,
> that we, being dead to sins, should live unto righteousness:
> by whose stripes ye were healed. For ye were as sheep going
> astray; but are now returned unto the Shepherd and Bishop
> of your souls." (I Peter 2:24-25)

Everything must be understood within proper context; that is the most basic principle of scriptural understanding. Otherwise, massive confusion results, as is seen today in the erroneous Dominion proclamation that the church has now replaced historical Israel and all the promises of God's covenant nation now apply not to the Jews, but to us. Without proper context, the interpretive playing field is wide open.

Even a cursory examination of I Peter 2:24-25 indicates the apostle Peter is referencing the atonement and full forgiveness of sins. It has nothing whatever to do with the removal of sickness from the believer. The "healed" portion of the verse again is referencing every Christian being redeemed (healed) from the curse of sin, and the eternal punishment it warrants.

Further understanding is gained from a quick look at the Old Testament verse to which Peter had referred:

> But he was wounded for our transgressions, he was bruised for our iniquities: the chastisement of our peace was upon him; and with his stripes we are healed. All we like sheep have gone astray; we have turned every one to his own way; and the LORD hath laid on him the iniquity of us all. (Isaiah 53:5-6)

The context of this passage deals with the Suffering Servant, Christ Jesus, being a sacrifice for the sins of the world. Read on. The rest of the same chapter deals with the sin issue and Christ's blood atonement, not the healing of a person's physical body. We have altered this Old Testament promise of forgiveness of sins, and made it to be a panacea for all our physical ills instead.

One more New Testament verse bears close examination. Used extensively both in our congregation and Word of Faith groups, it does seem to promise healing of every sickness and offer the endowment of divine health. Again, context plays an important part in understanding the text:

> When the even was come, they brought unto him many that were possessed with devils: and he cast out the spirits with his

word, and healed all that were sick: That it might be fulfilled
which was spoken by Esaias the prophet, saying, Himself took
our infirmities, and bare our sicknesses. (Matthew 8:16-17)

Again, the scripture references the 53rd chapter of Isaiah, verse four:

Surely he hath borne our griefs, and carried our sorrows: yet
we did esteem him stricken, smitten of God, and afflicted.

Now, the word "griefs" in this passage does mean sickness, and
therefore it did prophesy the healing ministry of our Lord. But—and
this is critical—the New Testament indicates that the prophecy was
fulfilled where Matthew states, "That it might be fulfilled which was
spoken by Esaias the prophet."

This prophecy was fulfilled in Christ, in a set time and place,
and cannot be used as a blank check for ongoing divine health in a
believer. Again, Word of Faith teachers have taken out of context a
prophecy of the earthly ministry of Christ that validated his claim as
Messiah, and have applied it to Christians. And, not to every Christian,
mind you, but only those who will have faith according to Word of
Faith tenets.

Can we honestly believe that no one in the New Testament Church
ever got sick? Isn't that the Word of Faith meaning of divine health? In
fact, that is exactly what they teach. Not only should you never be sick,
many of them state, but Christians should live out their full hundred and
twenty years (Genesis 6:3) and only die by consent when those years are
fulfilled. At New Covenant, we heard the same repetitive propaganda.
Regular healing sessions after a Sunday or midweek service, punctuated
by the recipients of prayer being slain in the spirit, served to verify in
our own hearts that this doctrine was genuine. True to form, virtually
any teaching, if accompanied by the standard "signs and wonders,"
was adhered to by our congregation. Experience validated teaching.
Warnings from the Word of God notwithstanding, manifestations
took continuous precedence over the Scriptures we claimed to believe
but never understood.

Coming Into "Alignment"

Back in about the early '90s, we went through a series of divine healing videos put out by Charles and Francis Hunter, or "The Happy Hunters." At the end of each video, we put the teachings to the test—not the scriptural test for truth, mind you, but the 'practical application" of what we had just learned. By laying on of hands, usually administered by Jason but sometimes by others in the group, we often *felt* things—sometimes a sense like an electric current running through the body, sometimes "drunkenness" (I experienced this one time where I literally could not speak without slurring my words), and sometimes in a very strange manipulation of the limbs. This was particularly powerful. Once (and I was not the only one so affected), according to the command on the video, I stretched out my arms and brought my hands together in order to see if my back was out of alignment. Well, according to the Hunters' criteria it was, and when I asked for God to heal me, right there in that room with about fifteen other people, my back seemed to move of its own accord, my outstretched arms and shoulders slowly rotating as if there was another person inside me doing the motions. There appeared to be a definite power at work unlike any I had ever felt before. I was thrilled. Even elder Tom Smalley was impressed, pointing at me and exclaiming with a huge smile, "Look at Kevin!"

This manipulation went on for about ten minutes, when it gradually subsided and left altogether. We had seen many people on this video manifest in this way, so it was only natural that we should experience the same thing. Incidentally, I never did feel any lasting change in my back.

It wasn't my spine that needed aligning—it was my heart. And that needed to be aligned using the plumb line of God's Word. Although we could not find its precedent in Scripture, the experience was powerful, stimulating, and sometimes seemed to work. Even unbelievers who were occasionally brought to meetings testified of the power that coursed through their bodies and moved their limbs of its own accord. At least one, however, left our meeting hurting with worse pain than when he arrived.

Was it of God? What do you think? Its absence from the ministries of Jesus and the apostles should sound warning bells loud and clear.

This was a formula prayer, the same thing Jesus had in fact warned against in Matthew 6:7.

"Do this, and this will happen." How many times I heard that kind of spiritual reasoning in our congregation eludes me. But God simply doesn't act that way. Jesus healed differently for different people, based on heart attitude, not a specific agenda, method, or ritual. One of the main points of the video, which fell right into line with our own doctrine, was that Christians should not be suffering under sickness. Well, if we believe that, then we will have a very hard time explaining away the sickness of sincere believers like Timothy (I Timothy 5:23), Epaphroditus (Philippians 2:25-27), and Trophimus (II Timothy 4:20). In congregations today that follow these doctrines of men, the many who suffer sickness, sometimes chronically, are placed in the position of being healed or being condemned for their lack of faith, either by church leadership, the congregation, or their own feelings. They believe they have failed God. Or worse, that God has failed them.

Headed For the Reefs

I once corresponded with a man who had been in prison for a number of years, sentenced to hard time for armed robbery. He was born-again in prison and had a genuine heart to serve the Lord, but he had a chronic back condition that gave him regular pain and apparently inhibited his freedom of movement to the point that he could not exercise regularly. Unfortunately, he was given some Word of Faith material and cleaved to the teachings of Kenneth Copeland. He also subscribed to Voice of Victory material, put out by Copeland's ministry. After reading the instructions for some time, he took the teachings at face value, "confessed his healing" despite the steady pain, and even wrote asking me to pray a prayer along with him for thirty days, after which time God would certainly restore him to fullness of health. I hesitated to do this, as I had suffered many years from physical problems as well and was beginning to believe that God had His own plans regardless of our desires. But I reluctantly agreed, and for the next month, prayed for my brother's healing.

The prayer, which he had written out for me, went something like this:

> I thank you, Father, that I am healed by the stripes of Jesus Christ, and that you laid all sickness on Him. Thank you that sickness shall not have place in my body or my life, and that I am even now experiencing the health of Christ.

It went on, of course, but you get the idea—no petition, no humble requesting, merely the insistence that he was already healed because of the work of the atonement. I probably don't need to relate the outcome. My friend was not healed, and consequently grew very angry and accusative toward God. He blamed the Lord, not Kenneth Copeland. His faith floundered from that point, suffering near-shipwreck.

My friend's story is by no means the exception. I have known others personally whose faith was battered when God did not heal according to Word of Faith formulas. Their confidence in God was sorely shaken, and they have these doctrines and those promoting them to thank for it.

Some of us still remember the frightening book, *We Let Our Son Die,* in which the parents involved in a positive confession church group withheld life-giving insulin from their diabetic son.[6] The boy succumbed, and the grieving parents were thrown into the horrifying realization that God had no part in the tragedy. The father of the boy, Larry Parker, rose courageously to tell his own story as a warning to others.

When I mentioned wanting to lend this book out to others after having read it sometime in the mid-1990s, then-pastor Tom Smalley cautioned me against doing so. It might have a damaging effect on some people's faith, he said. In his mind, it was perhaps more dangerous to actually warn of destructive error than it was to let it go unchecked.

How many others have died because of religiously following Word of Faith formulas? As New Covenant Fellowship members, we were taught that sickness and physical pain were just a cover-up from Satan to rob us of our divine health. How many times I heard, "Don't believe your symptoms. Believe God!" I cannot count. One visiting minister repeatedly told us, "Your sickness is a fact; your healing is the truth." What is that supposed to mean? There *is* no difference between fact and truth. Christ's blood shed for the forgiveness of my sins is a fact, and it is also the truth. His resurrection is both.

As far as the demon factor is concerned, while it is true that the devil and demons can inflict sickness on the body of a Christian, it is not always their doing. And while the promises of God are real and supernaturally powerful, claiming absolute perfect health all the time is just not possible this side of heaven. We forget that we live in a fallen world. *People who live here get sick.* There's no crime in admitting that. In fact, it can bring great release to a chronic pain sufferer. After being told for years that it was *his fault* that he wasn't healed, or that he didn't have enough faith for his diabetic daughter to throw away the insulin, what freedom for a poor beleaguered soul to realize that sickness in this life is just part of the package!

Quadriplegics like Joni Eareckson Tada present a great problem to the Word of Faith camp. They are in fact an embarrassment because, according to Word/Faith doctrine, either they are in sin or their faith is too weak to effect healing. And don't kid yourself—there are lots of us out there, folks who have been pummeled senseless by this teaching on top of having to struggle with the daily physical pain of chronic illness. How many have walked away from faith in Christ because they just couldn't take it anymore—no one will ever know until the accounting at the end of the age.

The dangerous nature of this doctrine is exemplified in an occurrence at New Covenant. Sometime in the early '90s, the husband of one of our members began suffering from recurrent, blinding head pain. Jason went to pray for him, and supposedly saw a vision of an octopus-like demon with tentacles wrapped around the man's brain. Whenever it squeezed one of the tentacles, Jason said, the man had tremendous pain, which sometimes knocked him to the floor. Jason rebuked the "demon," but the man was not healed. He was shortly thereafter diagnosed with a brain tumor. Surgical removal of the cancerous growth provided immediate relief, and he is doing well today as a prominent member of our community.

The moral of this story should be obvious. It wasn't a demon causing the pain. You can't surgically remove a demonic spirit. The simple
fact is that a brain tumor had developed and needed to be extricated.
The scary part is that the man could easily have died had he heeded the
supposed word of knowledge and the imagined vision of our pastor.
At the time, Jason was insistent about the accuracy of his revelation,
and despite the glaring evidence, I never heard any public refutation
of it or apology to the congregation for the vision's fraudulent nature.
I witnessed this practice over and over in our congregation.

If something doesn't work, or proves embarrassingly contrary to
the situation's outcome, simply ignore it. Hush it up, and the congregation will eventually forget.

But should it be this way? Why be afraid to bring failure out into
the cleansing light of Christ (John 3:20-21, I John 1:7)? Months before
I left our congregation of twelve years, my pastor's wife told me that
her greatest fear was that I would go public with what I knew and had
seen. She was concerned about the possible division such revelations
(which she believed were my own interpretation) might bring. But such
reasoning should not even be an issue. What happens in our church
groups should be out in the open for anyone to see. Personal confession of sin aside, secrecy has no place in the body of Christ.

Although a definite hierarchy of power prevailed, with Jason being at the top of the pyramid, I think his motive in preaching all these
things was to lead us into a more full relationship with God. There
factors in, however, an undeniable attitude of superiority, reflected in
the prevailing mindset of both leadership and membership that, as a
congregation, we were on the cutting-edge of what God was doing
in the world. As far as we were concerned, the other congregations
around town were missing out.

After all, when you believe that the fullness of the Godhead
dwells *in you* in bodily form, a pronounced sense of superiority is the
only reasonable outcome.

Chapter 2

Demons, Demons Everywhere

*"You walked in here with one. He was bigger than you,
and you didn't even know it."*

I sat wide-eyed in a chair in the New Covenant Fellowship office, a small cubicle located in the basement of our local clinic. Jason Klein stood with his back to me, drawing diagrams on an erasable marker board, turning periodically to face me and make sure I understood what he was saying.

I had entered the office only a moment earlier to spend a few minutes in conversation with my pastor, blissfully unaware of the "revelation" that was to follow. When I walked in, Jason had been standing at the front of the little room, engaged in something or other, and the instant he laid eyes on me his entire demeanor grew solemn. He turned sharply, and with his back to me began speaking as he outlined on the marker board at the front of the room what he "discerned in his spirit." At first I was confused, for he did not immediately come right out and say so, but I soon realized he was saying that a demon had attached itself to me and was following me around, influencing my thoughts and actions. I became alarmed, especially when Jason noted that the being (which I supposed he had visibly seen) loomed taller than most men. The diagrams he drew showed that the demon was connected to me, with instructions on how to get rid of it.

And get rid of it we did. I hastily renounced any involvement that may have brought this spirit into my life, and I left the building happy I was "cleansed."

Everybody Has One

An unhealthy fascination with demons was always at the core of New Covenant practice. Since we were a "power" church group, we were initiated into a lengthy course on demonology: the identities of various demons, how they manifest themselves in the life of the average Christian, and how we could combat them. Of course, it was a given that we had the authority to wage war, since Christ dwelt in us, and we were to do the works of our Lord. But it was nearly always taken to ludicrous extremes. While the believer in Christ does have the authority to cast out demons, it was never Jesus' intent to have His disciples dwell on the spirit beings of darkness and invent new ways to deal with them. As a congregation who believed in deliverance, Jason felt it necessary to offer basic, intermediate, and advanced instruction on confronting the demonic.

In our learning, we "discovered" that a wide variety of demons confronted the believer, armed with a bewildering array of "assignments" against his Christian enemy. While demons of sickness were common, prominent among other "classes" of demons were "religious spirits" and "generational spirits." The duty of the religious class was to make sure Christians became bound up in empty tradition, devoid of any real relationship with Christ. The Pharisees of Jesus' day were a prime example, we were told. Nominal Christians also fell into this category. Oddly, even genuine believers could be bound up by a religious demon if they adhered only to the Word of God and did not accept teachings outside its boundaries. Refusal to accept any manifestation, originating within a *church* context, however bizarre, was nearly always chalked up to either immaturity or having a religious spirit, which blinded the person to a true work of God. This teaching was part and parcel of our understanding, and was liberally applied by us to other congregations in town, simply because they disagreed with our methods and beliefs.

It's In the Genes

Generational spirits were often blamed for a believer's perceived inability to overcome certain besetting sins like alcoholism, adultery, or cursing. The idea was that a certain demonic assignment, carried out by a particular spirit far back in a person's family history, was passed down from generation to generation, bringing with it the same destructive mission it had visited upon a person's ancestors. A believer under the influence of (or inhabited by) this kind of demon was looked upon as nearly helpless in the face of temptation, reaping the wild oats sown by an errant forefather deep in the past. It is a form of spiritual heredity. The scripture used to justify this thinking was paraded forth so often it became a standard:

> And the LORD passed by before him, and proclaimed, The LORD, The LORD God, merciful and gracious, long-suffering, and abundant in goodness and truth, Keeping mercy for thousands, forgiving iniquity and transgression and sin, and that will by no means clear the guilty; visiting the iniquity of the fathers upon the children, and upon the children's children, unto the third and to the fourth generation. (Exodus 34:6-7)

On the face of it, a generational legacy seems to make a great deal of sense, but if we back up a bit to Exodus 20:5, we find God has already stated the situation with clarity: "…visiting the iniquity of the fathers upon the children unto the third and fourth generation *of them that hate me*" (emphasis mine). And also in Ezekiel 18:1-4:

> The word of the LORD came unto me again, saying, What mean ye, that ye use this proverb concerning the land of Israel, saying, The fathers have eaten sour grapes, and the children's teeth are set on edge? As I live, saith the Lord GOD, ye shall not have occasion any more to use this proverb in Israel. Behold, all souls are mine; as the soul of the father, so also the soul of the son is mine: the soul that sinneth, it shall die.

It stands to reason that if the head of a family is a hater of God, then he will automatically pass that belief system down to his offspring. With some people, we see that kind of legacy in their daily lives. Certainly God will visit their iniquity upon them, for they have already been taught to hate the Lord and despise His ways. But to insist that a Christian, a completely new creation, is bound by those same ancestral sins is ludicrous and does violence to the very grace of God:

> In those days they shall say no more, The fathers have eaten a sour grape, and the children's teeth are set on edge. But every one shall die for his own iniquity: every man that eateth the sour grape, his teeth shall be set on edge. (Jeremiah 31:29-30)

> Therefore if any man be in Christ, he is a new creature: old things are passed away; behold, all things are become new." (II Corinthians 5:17)

Let's look at this sensibly—if Christ delivered us from the very condemnation of hell by our simply receiving Him (John 1:12) through grace, would He then leave any smaller matter undone? Would He allow His child to be tormented by a demonic spirit for years because of the sins committed by an unknown ancestor or family leader? Remember, the moment we believe on Christ for salvation, we are no longer under the tyranny of evil. We have been brought into a new kingdom:

> Who hath delivered us from the power of darkness, and hath translated us into the kingdom of his dear Son." (Colossians 1:13)

The fact is, there is not one mention of a generational spirit in the entire Bible. It is another bit of Christian mythology that has entered a gate of error left wide open by removing the vigilant gatekeeper, the Word of God.

Familiarity Breeds Contempt

One book in particular passed around in our congregation was called simply, *Familiar Spirits*, or something to that effect. This soft cover volume explained that these are demons who are familiar with people, have access to their companionship, and can influence them without the person being aware of it. In actuality, the word *familiar* used here is taken from Leviticus 20:27 to indicate a medium or spiritist. A person who had a familiar spirit deliberately delved into the occult to contact the spirits of the dead.

In light of Scripture, to state that a believer bought with the blood of Christ has a familiar spirit is to basically label (libel) him as a necromancer who willingly cavorts with demons. This kind of spiritual interaction belongs to the realm of the notorious witch of Endor, as recorded in I Samuel 28:7-14. Assigning Christians to this abominable category is horrible biblical interpretation, insulting to the Lord who delivered us from the kingdom of darkness and redeemed us as citizens in His kingdom of light (Ephesians 5:8).

Nonetheless, it was openly accepted in our group that almost everyone had a familiar spirit, ourselves included. Prior to our salvation in Christ, we had all dabbled in various evil practices and were told that we had picked up demons that, until they were exorcised, would continue to harass us. Even church leadership had its share. I recall Tom Smalley relating the confrontation between Jason Klein and the supposed demons in Tom's wife, Sherri. When Jason came too close, Sherri put up her hands and backed away nervously, insisting that Jason keep his distance. "She's manifesting!" Jason had said.

Perhaps Sherri was appropriately nervous about Jason's crowding her personal space, a habit of his that more than once compelled *me* to avoid him.

A subsequent deliverance session involving Jason, Tom, and Sherri "confirmed" that two familiar spirits had taken up residence in Sherri since her childhood, waiting for the day she could be effectively schooled in witchcraft. Jason even described the appearance of one of the demons—an old woman. Sherri "broke off" agreement with these spirits, they were "cast out," and she was "free." This is only one example of many where those being "ministered to" were required to go through humiliation while the minister was elevated.

Delivering the Delivered

Deliverance was a key feature of New Covenant discussion, doctrine, and practice. It was also very frightening at times, but exciting and fascinating as well. It was always done on only one person at a time, prompted by either a recipient of "revelation knowledge" from someone in the congregation or the candidate demonstrating what we believed were the trademarks of demonization. The symptoms could be anything—depression, anxiety, anger, lust, perverse thoughts, even alcohol or cigarette addiction! Once the candidate agreed to the required procedure, he or she met with a group of usually about five members who had spent the day in prayer and perhaps fasting. With the demonized person in the center, the others crowded close and began to pray, often with the laying on of hands and speaking in other tongues. Then the "insights" began.

Sometimes demons took definite shape in the mind of the praying persons, or "simply manifested" in the candidate in any number of ways—excessive crying, moaning, violent shaking, jerking, anger, etc. One by one, the demons would be commanded to present themselves and disclose their assignments of darkness. A veritable list of … well, whatever … came forth from these supposed demonic entities. Assignments like lust, manipulation, lying … just about anything the person struggled with was labeled a demon. After what was often several hours of an exhausting process and amid much crying, fear, hugging, rejoicing, and praising the Lord, the person was pronounced delivered.

Some might argue that the uncontrollable jerking and convulsing (and other manifestations) that may have occurred is proof these individuals were demonically possessed. But this is only to confuse demonic possession with demonic activity. No doubt, there was demonic activity involved in our legitimizing an unscriptural practice and thereby participating in deception. But nowhere in Scripture do we find evidence that Christians can be demonically possessed. On

the contrary, Scripture shows that the Holy Spirit cannot co-habit
with a demon:

> What? know ye not that your body is the temple of the Holy
> Ghost which is in you, which ye have of God, and ye are
> not your own? (I Corinthians 6:19)

When any spirits of darkness came anywhere near Jesus, they cried
loudly that He is the Son of God (Mark 1:23-24, Matthew 8:29), they
fell writhing before him (Mark 9:20-26), they reacted in panic (Luke
8:28), and "every single one left." No demon could stand to be in
the holy presence of Christ. They knew who He was. They had once
been with Him in heaven and bowed at His feet. How could it now
be said that people whom God had purchased with His own blood
(Acts 20:28), a people whose consciences had been cleansed by that
same precious blood (Hebrews 9:14), and in whom dwells that same
Jesus by the Holy Spirit (Colossians 1:27), still have demons within
them? Has God left anything undone?:

> And ye are complete in him, which is the head of all prin-
> cipality and power. (Colossians 2:10)

Can a demon live in the same holy vessel in which resides the "head
of all principality and power"? Those who think so have some serious
rethinking to do.

It is interesting to note that there is no account in Scripture where
a demon is being cast out of a believer. Yet, when Paul talks about
besetting sins, his response is not to seek exorcism but to recognize
that the flesh (our human nature and depravity) can never please God
(Romans 8:8), and consequently we must confess our sins and allow
the Holy Spirit full reign over our lives (Romans 8:12-13).

In Ephesians 6:10-17, Paul acknowledges that we do battle against
the schemes of the devil, but his instructions on how to do this battle
is to stand firm: "Put on the whole armour of God, that ye may be
able to stand against the wiles of the devil (vs. 11). He later describes

how we are to engage in this spiritual warfare. Again, no mention of casting out demons is given, but the mandate to stand on the promises of God, firm in our faith and bearing the assurance of salvation found in Christ alone is.

The teaching used to get around this obvious discrepancy made exaggerated use of the tripartite nature of the human being. We were taught that the Holy Spirit dwells in us, but only in our spirit, leaving our physical bodies open to demonic habitation. But, even this contorted presentation is easily disallowed by I Corinthians 6:15-20. The verses are not speaking of our spirits, but our bodies. A reading in context offers a clear picture of what Paul is referring to:

> Know ye not that your bodies are the members of Christ? shall I then take the members of Christ, and make them the members of an harlot? God forbid. What? know ye not that he which is joined to an harlot is one body? for two, saith he, shall be one flesh. But he that is joined unto the Lord is one spirit. Flee fornication. Every sin that a man doeth is without the body; but he that committeth fornication sinneth against his own body. What? know ye not that your body is the temple of the Holy Ghost which is in you, which ye have of God, and ye are not your own? For ye are bought with a price: therefore glorify God in your body, and in your spirit, which are God's.

We are told not to dishonor our bodies with fornication, because they are the dwelling place of the Holy Spirit. This should put to rest once and for all any idea that our bodies may be divvied up by all spiritual takers.

Another major scriptural discrepancy with deliverance theology as taught by New Covenant (as well as much of the charismatic community) is that lust is not caused by demons, but rather by the sinful inclinations of the flesh as these verses state:

> But every man is tempted, when he is drawn away of his own lust, and enticed. Then when lust hath conceived, it

bringeth forth sin: and sin, when it is finished, bringeth forth
death. (James 1:14-15)

Now the works of the flesh are manifest, which are these;
Adultery, fornication, uncleanness, lasciviousness, idolatry,
witchcraft, hatred, variance, emulations, wrath, strife, sedi-
tions, heresies, envyings, murders, drunkenness, revellings,
and such like: of the which I tell you before, as I have also
told you in time past, that they which do such things shall
not inherit the kingdom of God. (Galatians 5:19-21)

Both James and Paul make it very clear it is the believer's responsibility to steer clear of these sins by keeping his own flesh under control.
These are sins of the flesh, indulged by desires contrary to the desires
of God. That we do have control, and are not at the whim of some
resident spirit of darkness, is stated by the apostle Paul:

There hath no temptation taken you but such as is common
to man: but God is faithful, who will not suffer you to be
tempted above that ye are able; but will with the temptation
also make a way to escape, that ye may be able to bear it. (I
Corinthians 10:13)

A believer in Christ Jesus is not powerless in temptation because
Jesus has taken up residence. But the premise of the modern deliverance ministry is the opposite, which states that a demon within the
person pulls the reins so to speak, and controls the outward actions
of the person being demonized.

Chauffeuring the Spirits

Tom Smalley said that very thing. Pastor Jason had revealed that
a demon following Tom around had hooked up reins to Tom's
thoughts and feelings, making Tom think they were his own. Every
time the demon wanted Tom to think in a certain way, he (the demon)
would just give a tug on the reins, directing Tom whichever way it best

suited the purposes of darkness. Of course, after Jason's revelation, Tom went ahead and renounced the demon, and it left. For years afterward, Tom spoke of this deliverance in an affirmative light.

For some time now, the idea has gained popular ground that we, as Christians, can unwittingly harbor and act as carriers for demonic entities in much the same way that one would pick up a virus. Now, we're not speaking of attacks by demons. Those are to be expected, but as we stand in Christ and follow Him, Scripture assures us that any angels of darkness coming against us have already been stripped of power by the victory of the Cross (Colossians 2:13-15). Our thinking can be influenced from the outside by doctrines of demons (I Timothy 4:1), and we can live accordingly, straying from the true faith. But what was practiced in New Covenant Fellowship was the doctrine that we can become somewhat of a chauffeur, driving around demons in a fleshly limousine and taking directions like a hired hand. This simply isn't biblical. It robs part of our inheritance, the liberty in which we stand in Christ Jesus. Given wide publicity and validated in Joyner's *The Final Quest*, this idea of controlling demons has rapidly gained in popularity emerging from the sidelines to become mainstream doctrine for hyper-charismatic Christians.

It cannot be stated too strongly how far this dangerous thinking can lead. Instead of taking responsibility for one's own thoughts and corresponding deeds, a demon is conveniently blamed. This excuse can run the gamut from overeating to adultery, or the whole range of sinful acts within Galatians 5, with the *victim* tearfully claiming inability to cease from sin. Modern deliverance practitioners, myself formerly included, would agree that as long as the demon was present, the person would suffer loss of control in some area of his or her life. It would be free to harass and wear down the sufferer until the sin was accomplished. I have personally heard of demons of nicotine, anger, self-pity, lust, homosexuality … just about anything a human being can get himself into. One of the most unusual (and embarrassing) demons I ever heard addressed was the spirit of halitosis! Jason "cast it out" of me during a meeting in the church office. Now, it should be obvious that I needed a bit more mouthwash on that particular day, but to blame it on the devil's henchman…

We need to get real here. The evasion of personal accountability is something the church has long had to deal with. Shirking responsibility began with Adam in the Garden of Eden. No one likes to admit and confess when caught in sin. But it is the only way to literally come clean. I John 1:9 is God's beautiful promise of forgiveness but only to those who admit and confess their sins: "If we confess our sins, he is faithful and just to forgive us our sins, and to cleanse us from all unrighteousness."

As believers, we experience wonderful liberation from sinful desires and actions in the confession of sin. We don't have to blame it on a demon. "Submit yourselves therefore to God. Resist the devil, and he will flee from you" (James 4:7). Why would James even bother with this command if our efforts were useless? Note that he doesn't say to get deliverance. He simply says resist!

The promised outcome is that "[H]e [the devil] will flee." It doesn't say he will hide out in your body until the next opportune moment. We must recognize the authority of the God-breathed Word or we will be forever stumbling around, using our own imaginations and presumed spiritual experiences to deal with what has already been dealt with at the Cross.

Murder by Demon

Jason once recounted an experience he had with a demon who tried to kill him. Awakened in the middle of the night by someone entering his bedroom, he turned to see the figure of a man crouched down beside the bed, with his head bowed as if in prayer. "Agree with me," the man said.

Becoming alarmed, Jason attempted to waken his wife Jessie, but she could not be stirred. Jason said he knew that this was a demon come to take his life. At about this point, Jason said his heart stopped. He felt his spirit leave his body and then looked down to see his prone figure on the bed. The upshot of the whole experience was that the demon eventually left, and Jason lived to tell the incident.

Did it actually happen? After everything that happened in New Covenant Fellowship, I simply cannot believe it. It may have been a dream, or perhaps not even that. There is no reference in the Bible to a person's spirit temporarily leaving the body, floating above it and looking down on his own lifeless corpse. John's experience on Patmos can hardly be used as a comparison, since he was taken to heaven and never in fact died. Paul's translation to the third heaven never involved his looking back at his dead body, if he was indeed dead. On the contrary, hovering above one's body sounds like first-hand stories told by practitioners of astral projection, an occult practice. The whole incident seemed to spotlight Jason and his frequent encounters with demons rather than the power of the living Lord.

Behind Every Rock and Bush

W ith a theological diet of this sort, emissaries of darkness became apparent everywhere. They were in houses, dark glades, bright living rooms, cars, and boats. One sister even believed a demon had taken up residence in her air conditioner. She based this observation on the practice our group once had of anointing with oil everything we wanted protected from demonic habitation or interference. This sweet lady, after anointing every other place in the house, believed that the demon had retreated to her air conditioner, where she simply couldn't dislodge it. She asked if I could come over and order it from the building. By that time, about six years into my stay at New Covenant, I had delved into some personal, enlightening Bible study on anointing oil and assured her that exorcism was unnecessary.

But who could blame her? After all the teaching we had received by those whom we assumed knew more than we did, it was only natural for her to put into practice such techniques that were supposed to work. Kris and I did. In our early days at New Covenant, we bought into the whole anointing craze and did our entire house—from basement to master bedroom. We paid special attention to "portals" like ventilation ducts, windows, and doors. These, we had been sagely informed by church leadership, were the entry ways into our home, the places demons were most likely to come through in order to set up shop. We never stopped to think that spirits of darkness, being incorporeal beings, are not bound by conventional methods of entry. Unencumbered with inconvenient flesh, they can easily pass through walls, roofing, or whatever section of a building suits them. Until the day we left that house for another, you could still see clearly the dried outline of oil-made crosses over certain doorways.

A Return to Medieval Superstition

Where did these ideas come from? Certainly not the Bible. Although Jacob's anointing of the rock and the Israelites' anointing with oil the implements of the tabernacle were sometimes cited as proof, these texts have nothing whatever to do with warding off demons. Biblically, only those things which were consecrated to the Lord's use were anointed, such as objects in the tabernacle used in worship and these were very few indeed. And they were anointed via instructions received directly from God.

Whenever we purchased something of dubious origin, usually from a garage sale, we made certain to claim it for the kingdom of God, commanding the demons to leave the object. Only then did we feel safe having it in our house, free of satanic influence. The purchase could have been anything—a book, a mirror, a radio—but they all underwent the same procedure. And again, with no scriptural warrant. A little history might help bring the man-made origins of this practice into sharper focus. If ever there was an evil group, it was the Philistines, and God often told the Israelites to gather up the plunder after the battle. No instruction was ever given to anoint the spoils of war and command attendant demons to flee.

It has been hard to admit, but this practice is rank superstition. Aside from being a colossal waste of time, it dishonored God, whose protection can certainly extend to a clock radio, no matter who the previous owner may have been. It is interesting to think that while we believed we were walking in power, we were ruled by fear. Rituals had to be done correctly and often in order to be effective. A slip-up and the demons could come back in force, able to harass us on a legal technicality.

One point of clarification here: objects used in witchcraft, Satanism, or any facet of the occult would be the exception, along with idols used in pagan worship. There is no legitimate reason, for instance, to bring objects like a Ouija board or tarot cards into a

Christian home. A miniature representation of a pagan god is not simply a piece of artwork, but an idol. Scripture calls these practices an abomination (Deuteronomy 18: 9-12), an affront to God which should be burned. The new believers in Ephesus had the right idea (Acts 19: 18-19).

You See What?

Visions of demons were often at the forefront at New Covenant. We based much of our understanding of the kingdom of darkness on what our members supposedly saw in the spirit. One sister had a vision of a small imp sitting on the shoulder of her friend. The diminutive demon's assignment was to disrupt communication. Whenever this sister spoke to her friend, the imp would grab her words out of the air, twist them into a convoluted shape, and then stuff them into her friend's head. The outcome of this, of course, was that her friend became angry when she misinterpreted the words. Not to be outdone, Jason stated that once, in response to specific prayer to be able to see Satan, he was rewarded when the god of this age actually appeared before him, exuding the full horror of his evil nature.

Bizarre though they were, there were many reported visions of this kind among our membership. Such vivid and recurrent imagery guided us deeper into an esoteric knowledge strictly opposed to traditional Christianity. Quite frankly, the Scriptures went one way, and we went another. We considered experience critical. If one member of our congregation *saw* a demon, the validity of the experience was already assumed. After all, we were Christians, and it happened in a church service, a special meeting, or during prayer. What else could it be, we reasoned, but God revealing these things to us?

Kris and I had some encounters with darkness that were real, and overcame them in the name of Jesus. However, because we had strayed far from the true Gospel, genuine spiritual confrontations were most likely in the *very rare* category. But I recall a few instances in my own walk when I am convinced Christ demonstrated His true power, and demons did flee.

On Close Examination

Prove all things; hold fast that which is good.
(I Thessalonians 5:21)

W e examined virtually nothing. We didn't need to, remember? We were in church, and only good things happen in church. We held fast, not only to that which we knew to be good, but to that which *appeared* good. And what seemed good often appealed to our quest for power and wisdom.

At this point, I would like to make something very clear. Our congregation was not a bad lot. We were a praying people with giving, loving hearts. The townspeople recognized our joy as we witnessed to anyone who would listen. Although we suffered a certain amount of ridicule and opposition even from other Christian groups, it was generally acknowledged that we loved the sinner and reached out to the hurting. For the most part, we genuinely desired to see the kingdom of God advanced on the earth and multitudes saved. Our love for each other was evident, and in some measure that I haven't quite figured out yet, I believe we truly loved the Lord.

Hindsight is generally a perfect 20/20, so I now recognize we had a hunger for the sensational, a one-upmanship in relation to the other Christian groups in town. Sure, Kris and I would witness to people, but often it was with the attached motive to bring them to New Covenant Fellowship. Certainly we'd want a convert to be raised up in the best teaching in the valley, and that meant our group, hands down. Dreams, visions, powerful manifestations, head-on confrontations with the kingdom of darkness—who wouldn't want to be a part of all that?

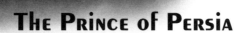

CHAPTER 3

THE PRINCE OF PERSIA

"We say to the spirit of the North, give up those whom you have been
hindering from entering into the kingdom of God!"

Following the pattern set out in the Larry Lea video series, *Could
You Not Tarry One Hour?*,[1] our early morning gathering stood with
fingers pointing and voices raised. At the front of the small rented
church office, Jason led us off with "warfare" praying and then into
direct conflict with the supposed immense demonic spirit holding
unbelievers captive. According to the video presentation, this black-
as-night demon covered with moss grasped with huge hands the
chains that shackled people to their false belief systems. We believed
him to be the principal spirit of the geographical North. As spiritual
commandos, our job was to get in his face and in the name of Jesus
order him to release the chains so unbelievers could experience salvation. Once he had backed off because of his fear of our authority,
we commanded the angels of God to go and minister salvation and
bring those newly released into the kingdom of God.

It didn't end with the North. All four cardinal points of the compass each had its own gargantuan spirit or principality that needed
combating before people could enter the kingdom. With our warfare
and the hosts of angels responding to our commands, multitudes
would be saved.

Larry Lea said it would happen. He had led a huge gathering of people
into this same kind of prayer, and we had watched his entire video series

in one of our elders' homes a few nights running. In fact, so powerful was the video and prayer that when Lea said, "There it is!" (referring to the chain-holding demon spirit), I was too afraid to look.

Where Did the Idea Come From?

This practice, supposedly supported by a text from Isaiah 43:5-6, seemed to give us a blank check to rescue people from the bondage of Satan. But look at the entire passage in its full and proper context by starting in verse one: it is *God*, not we, who calls for the North to give up. And He's not even addressing a demon. Besides, it is His sons and daughters, not unbelievers, whom He summons from the various geographical points. *Plus*, the complete context of the chapter seems strongly to indicate that God's command has to do with returning the people of Israel to their homeland after they suffer worldwide dispersion.

In a word, the primary verse used as foundation for this belief and practice has nothing at all to do with warring "in the heavenlies."

Let's Pick Up the Sword!

Few other doctrines have gained as much respectability in the last decade as this new type of spiritual warfare: *spiritual mapping.* Crossing denominational lines, this teaching has gathered together a veritable army of adherents, all with the express purpose of freeing individual towns, cities, and even nations from the bondage of Satan and his demonic *rulers, powers, and world forces of this darkness* (Ephesians 6:12). Through a set of specific rituals, the teaching goes, unbelievers can have the blindness lifted from their eyes in order to receive the truth, crimes plaguing an area will come to a miraculous halt, and Christians will see conversions, en masse, to the Gospel.

The core membership of our congregation learned a great deal about spiritual warfare from New Covenant's founder. What Jason Klein told us made sense, using a weave of Scriptures to form a doctrine that at least had a quality veneer. Although the pattern proved in time to be hopelessly moth eaten, it was all so exciting. Who wouldn't want to be in on the biggest military operation geared toward setting the people of our valley free from Satan's influence? And military it was. Jason himself had said that the church office would be the base of operations from which sorties against our demonic enemies would be conducted. Like commandos in a hit-and-run guerrilla war, we would strike without warning and scatter the forces of darkness arrayed against the kingdom of God.

The *Redeeming the Land* incident that I related early in my book (page 15) was only the first *military* step in our war.

Mountaintop Experiences

High places also topped the list of area raids. Since Old Testament false gods were worshipped on the peaks and plateaus surrounding a particular locality, we reasoned that the spirits of those false gods still liked being there. Looking down on our community, they had, we believed, the power to act with impunity. As long as our local high places hadn't been redeemed, the valley would likely not be set free. Some of our group had gone to the pinnacles around our town, but what went on there I can only assume on the basis of our motives.

I was jealous at the time for not being in on some of those particular counter-attacks. I yearned to be even more a part of power encounters and, along with my brothers and sisters, break the curses that had held our townspeople in spiritual blindness. We believed we were doing something tremendous, and at times the feeling was nothing short of intoxicating.

Digging Up the Roots

An integral part of spiritual mapping was discovering past events that occurred on specific plots of land. If any piece of real estate was suspect (and they *all* seemed to be at the time), a little research always confirmed some dark deed committed there such as murder, witchcraft, etc. With the area thus found to be "cursed," it was our job to liberate it. Always this involved the confession of the sins done there and asking God's forgiveness. Now, we need to understand this: we did not confess *our own sins*, but those of past transgressors. Supposedly, it was these particular sins that had allowed the resident demons to lay legal claim to the ground—in some cases for hundreds of years. Bringing the sins out in the open exposed the demons to the light of the truth, and loosened their hold. Although I went along with it, I never did understand how we could ask forgiveness for sins committed by someone we didn't even know. I always figured it was his responsibility, not ours, and if the transgressor was long dead as was often the case, confession on his behalf was too late. Eternal judgment for sin is executed at the moment of death (Hebrews 9:27).

There is brief mention in Scripture of some of the Old Testament saints confessing the sins of backslidden Israel, but they have nothing to do with breaking some presumed curse on a specified land mass. And their sins were not enumerated, as our congregation was wont to do. Neither did they research the land's history to discover specific sins that had defiled the land. Instead, there was wholesale, nationwide repentance.

The fact that each man answers for his own sin is recorded loud and clear in Ezekiel 18:20:

> The soul that sinneth, it shall die. The son shall not bear the iniquity of the father, neither shall the father bear the iniquity of the son: the righteousness of the righteous shall be upon him, and the wickedness of the wicked shall be upon him.

And just what would an uninitiated person watching from the shadows have thought about this kind of Christian convocation? What thoughts would flood my mind should I today stumble across a similar meeting? The eerie atmosphere of group-praying in a secluded wood lot, often in the dark of night, over the evil deeds of persons unknown and perhaps centuries in the grave, conjures up the archived images of grade B horror films.

The theme of *identificational repentance* is at the heart of the popular *reconciliation walks* touted throughout the hyper-charismatic realm at present.[2] The idea is that, by walking in parade-fashion with Muslims, Native Americans, or others of various world faiths, we

Christians can humble ourselves and repent for the sins our ancestors committed against the ancestors of these groups. Only then
will their eyes be opened to receive the good news of the gospel.
But, if it was not the method of the most determined evangelists in
history (the apostles), then it should have no place in our practice.
To proceed with such a formula, no matter how good it appears
on the outside, is to court spiritual disaster. History is replete with
examples of once-godly men and women taking things into their
own hands, based on some revelation, and tumbling off the ledge
into the deep abyss of heresy.

Strategic Bombing

As with our struggle with demons of a more intimate nature, oil
became incredibly important in our warfare against the higher-
ranking devils. Like a spiritual explosive, it was sprinkled liberally
on anything we wanted to blast free from the "curse" of the enemy.
Identified as a stronghold for Native American-oriented spirits of
darkness, an isolated river valley a few miles distant was targeted for,
literally, an air raid. The location was one of strong Native belief, and
historically, fear kept many, both white and Native, away from the
area. One of the wealthier members of our congregation, as pilot of
his own airplane, took off from the town's small airfield, with Pastor
Jason as a passenger. In Jason's lap was a balloon filled with anointing oil. The plan was to get right over the valley, open the cockpit
window, and release the spiritual cargo. The resultant impact was to
do great damage to the kingdom of darkness' power over the valley.
Nearing the area, the plane became buffeted by high winds, which
were attributed to spirits attacking the aircraft with the intent of
thwarting the mission. Not recalling the outcome of the story, I can
only assume that the balloon was dropped, but I can affirm that no
change came over the area. As far as the winds are concerned, when
I related the tale to a lifelong resident, she exclaimed incredulously,
"Why of course there are high winds there. They come right off the
glaciers that are all over those mountains!"

I had taken a boat ride with a friend into the area once, and sure enough, even low down on the water the winds were tremendous. They still are.

Let's Take a Walk

P*rayer walking* also became a prominent pastime for a number of us. Walking the streets while praying over homes and entire neighborhoods was supposed to free the inhabitants from the bondages of the devil. We prayed for people to have the blindness removed from their spiritual eyes so that they could see the Gospel of Jesus Christ, but I never did personally knock on anyone's door and actually *tell* them the good news of salvation. Neither did anyone else I know. Prayer walking is just that—walking and praying. I guess we would have taken the opportunity if someone had stepped outside his home and asked us, but it never presented itself. While there is nothing wrong with walking and praying simultaneously, to incorporate into it a rebuking of demonic spirits covering the spiritual eyes and ears of a specific family or neighborhood is to drastically overstep the bounds of a believer's authority and dabble in a realm of which we know little. Christ simply did not commission us to do this.

This concept of walking and praying is not limited to the individual Christian. It is carried out on a massive scale in many parts of the world. The *March for Jesus*, in which our group participated yearly, was birthed with the premise that war was being made in the heavenlies.[3] Contrary to its veneer of evangelism and love for the Lord, the *March* was a warfare maneuver designed to radically alter the balance of power in the spiritual realm. It was basically a "reclaiming the land" assault.

Doorways of Demons

G*ateways* were also the object of much concerted prayer and watchfulness on the part of our congregation. Any avenue of transportation into our valley was considered a highway whereby demonic entities could gain entrance and set up shop. Three main portals that exist here in our area—the state ferry system, the small airport, and the one road out of town—were all candidates for intensive, warrior-style prayer. It was felt that we could set up a situation in the heavenly places that would make it impossible for further demon immigration into our little river valley. Correspondingly, crime would then drop, religious fervor would increase, and many would be born into the kingdom of God. Actually, the reverse has happened. Despite our enormous effort in time and energy, drug and alcohol use among teens has gone up, all the bars and liquor stores are thriving, local governmental abuse has become a byword, and our town has gained notoriety as a Mecca for New Age practitioners of every stripe. As for the churches bursting at the seams—well, we won't even go there.

It should be obvious at this point that there is no scriptural foundation for any of these practices. It simply is not there. While it is true that "the god of this world hath blinded the minds of them which believe not" (II Corinthians 4:4), we have neither authority nor mandate from God to address Satan in this manner. All we are told is simply to preach the Gospel. Those who receive the Word of God will be saved, and those who do not are under condemnation. The fact is, anyone who truly wants to be saved can be:

> And the Spirit and the bride say, Come. And let him that heareth say, Come. And let him that is athirst come. And whosoever will, let him take the water of life freely. (Revelation 22:17)

> And ye shall seek me, and find me, when ye shall search for me with all your heart. (Jeremiah 29:13)

Where in the world do we get this idea that a big demon sits at each point of the compass, holding great chains that have bound unbelievers from receiving the Gospel? A thorough search of Scripture holds no such revelation. And as for rebuking the "territorial spirits" over an area, why didn't Paul do that before preaching at the Areopagus in Athens?:

> Now while Paul waited for them at Athens, his spirit was stirred in him, when he saw the city wholly given to idolatry. Therefore disputed he in the synagogue with the Jews, and

with the devout persons, and in the market daily with them
that met with him.… And they took him, and brought him
unto Areopagus, saying, May we know what this new doctrine, whereof thou speakest, is? (Acts 17: 16, 17, 19)

It's All in the Wrist

In the spiritual warfare power trip, technique is everything. My
former congregation believed if we worked the formula properly, the revival we prayed for would be ushered in full-blown. If
Paul in Athens had been using the techniques we have available
today, a quick glance at surrounding statues would have revealed
to him the ruling spirits. He could have bound and rebuked them,
commanded them to release their captives, and only *then* preached
the Gospel.

Using the logic of the spiritual mapping movement (i.e., the only
way to free an entire locality), it follows that since Paul knew nothing
of these practices, his effectiveness must have been greatly hindered.
Was the writer of half the New Testament deficient in the pursuit
of real evangelism, being unacquainted with methods revealed to the
church almost 2,000 years later? That poses the question of why God
would have withheld such information from the former persecutor of
the church, and from Barnabas, Peter, Stephen, and the other leaders
of the New Testament Church.

Winning souls would have become much easier had they concentrated on "bringing down strongholds and principalities in high
places" rather than merely speaking directly to people's hearts.

The discrepancies between current and biblical practices should
be painfully apparent. No, Paul didn't use any of the techniques so
popular today. Neither did any of the other apostles, nor Jesus for
that matter. If *anyone* could have taken a city for the kingdom of God,
it was the very Son of God. But these ideas, given credence by such
high-powered ministers as C. Peter Wagner,[4] find no precedent in
the entire canon of Scripture. Some congregations have even begun
driving stakes, anointed with oil, into the ground at various strategic
locations around the perimeter of their towns and cities, in hopes of

keeping out all demonic spirits. Listen—if there is any place in the world free of demons, I want to live there!

It's just not that easy. People have to get their hands dirty. Gospel proclamation is a one-on-one commitment to people and involvement with their lives. It is usually a painfully slow process, often with many setbacks. But our microwave mentality demands instant success, bypassing the only recorded methods that have proven effective in winning souls to our Lord.

Arrogance and Battle Fatigue

Involvement with this form of spiritual warfare takes its toll. While puffing up the participant with self-proclaimed authority, it also robs him of the real power of the Gospel message. While battling cosmic-sized opponents, the involved believer misses the down-to-earth battles with the flesh and yes, individual demonic hindrances of a less grandiose scale. And the sad reality of all the fuss is that it wastes massive amounts of time that could be spent in living the simple Christian walk before men.

Predictably, a sense of superiority marks those involved. During the early phases of my research, I telephoned my pastor (then Phil Clayton) to speak about this issue. As he was not home at the time, I spoke with his wife. When I remarked that *redeeming the land* warfare is nowhere found in the Bible, she became flustered. "So what if Jesus and the disciples didn't practice it!" she said. "It works!"

So, the bottom line becomes apparent—if something works, then it is of God. Based on that criterion, members of such worldwide cults as Jehovah's Witnesses and Mormons would be classed as part of the Christian community. Many involved in these Christless organizations lead exemplary lives and win converts. The importance of family, church, and country plays a big part in their daily walk. Yet, for all that, they are not saved.

Furthermore, if we're going to look at results, spiritual warfare of this nature *does not* work. In all the years my congregation battled "in the heavenlies," we did not change the character of our town one iota. Even areas we proclaimed free, complete with massive anointing of oil and a celebration of communion with dancing, kept on being used for the same profane purposes as before. Nationally, abortion is at an all-time high, divorce has shot through the proverbial roof, sexual perversion has scaled exotic new heights, and much of the church in North America has been sucked into a plethora of false experiences that result in an utter disregard for the Word of God. That does not match the dictionary definition of success.

It often appears that success is in the mind of the believer. If something is exciting, promotes unity on common ground (battling the enemy), and especially if it is wrapped up in supposed power, there will be no lack of participants. While the sincerity of most involved is probably genuine, fervent belief is no safeguard against the fraudulent. We must settle, once and for all, that every spiritual experience and practice must be measured against the Word of God. If a practice or doctrine is not in the Word, it must be discounted for safety's sake. Otherwise, the playing field becomes immeasurably broad. With no definite perimeters to bump up against, subjectivism rules the day, with an ever increasing yearning to top the last spiritual experience. Personal preference then becomes the final arbiter, and spiritual anarchy rages throughout the body of Christ. Instead of being ruled by the objective Word of God, we become like the spiritually bankrupt sons of Israel after the days of Joshua, when "every man did that which was right in his own eyes" (Judges 17:6).

Although Tom Smalley in later years sometimes vaguely cautioned against engaging in "weird" spiritual warfare tactics, his comments contained no specific mention of our own group's history of involvement, nor did he biblically repudiate such practices. He still held certain high-level ministers in great esteem and continued to preach their doctrines despite their international reputation in spiritual warfare circles, which made his occasional pulpit warnings appear so contradictory as to warrant disregard.

Middle East Strong Man

In the late 1980s, with a little band of like-minded believers, Jason journeyed to the Muslim nation of Iraq. The mission—to bring down the Prince of Persia (something they based on Daniel 10: 12-13).

The angel speaking with Daniel refers to the difficulty he had with a spiritual adversary, the Prince of Persia. It seems fair to assume that, since no human being can hold back an angelic being, the angel's opponent must have been a demon, perhaps one of the rulers spoken about in Ephesians 6:12. But Daniel's prayers did not assist the angel. Instead, despite Daniel's fervent plea, the angel was not able to respond for three weeks. It took another angelic prince, Michael, to come to the aid of this heavenly messenger. We must be careful to let the Scriptures be silent where God has ordained silence.

Jason had decided, through intense prayer and direct revelation, that it was necessary to battle the principalities over Iraq. That country's sadistic ruler, Saddam Hussein, held his people in an iron fist. Immense paintings of Hussein echoed his insatiable appetite for grandeur. One particular painting portrayed him receiving the ancient Babylonian code from Nebuchadnezzar. Jason said this painting not only showed that Hussein's leadership was in line with Nebuchadnezzar's, but that the ancient ruler of Babylon had actually passed along the baton of spiritual power to Hussein as well.

And this was the crux of Jason's visit. The biblical city of Babylon was still in the throes of demonic manipulation. Always noted in the Scriptures as the hotbed of abomination due to the worship of pagan deities, Babylon was key in world affairs. I suppose Jason believed that only an infiltration, a spiritual swat team, could make a dent in the power of the realm of darkness there.

The group was overseas for two or three weeks, and upon returning announced victory. Within two years, Jason said, events would come about to topple Saddam Hussein. The four-man team brought back slides that depicted the spiritual depravity of the Iraqi people. Photographs of the Gate of Ishtar, dedicated to the Babylonian false goddess of fertility, and even an ancient painting that resembled the Statue of Liberty, fascinated our congregation. As a fellowship of believers, we were so proud of them. They had faced what few would, had striven in prayer, and succeeded in their God-ordained mission. Or so it seemed.

It took courage for these men to go overseas into a desert land ruled by a maniacal dictator hostile to both Americans and Christianity. No doubt their prayers for protection and guidance were fervent. God in His mercy brought them home. But Saddam Hussein didn't fall until more than a decade later, and a quick scan of the U.S.-Iraq crisis up to the present indicates things in Iraq have only gotten worse. Christians and Jews have suffered severe ongoing persecution and martyrdom in countries like this where the Koran's teachings are enforced.

My former pastor believed God had sent him and his little group to war against demonic hosts and the ruling spirit they thought held sway over the ancient land of Persia. But not only is such thinking incredibly prideful, it is equally presumptuous. To insist that Saddam Hussein's political demise hinged on a team of intercessors who received immediate and direct revelation from God for this titanic battle is to grasp for power way beyond anything to be found in the pages of the Bible. And we all did it. As much as we spoke about personal holiness, power was still a key goal in our congregation. Power to heal, cast out demons … and war against principalities and powers. But that's what happens when people detour from clear biblical teaching to follow what they believe is the Holy Spirit, Who, in truth, always confirms the Scriptures. The voice, impression, leading—whatever—becomes the final arbiter. Scripture is put on the back burner, or made to fit the experience via a set of proof texts.

And the result is always calamitous.

CHAPTER 4

WE ALL FALL DOWN

"I saw the Lord Jesus coming to rest on you!"

Jason had just picked himself up from the floor at the front of the sanctuary and clasped the aged hands of a dear older believer who occasionally came to Sunday service. With a deep reverence, he gently kissed her hands in a gesture of honor.

Only a moment before he had been laid out on the carpet. Sister Carmen had come up front at the service's end to receive healing prayer for eyes suffering from progressive vision deterioration. She was a sweet old lady, a pioneer who talked a lot about getting back to her home in a small community farther north and deeper into the backcountry. In the previous few months, I had spent considerable time with her and her young companion, a fervent Christian and fellow sticks-dweller who had land staked out for homesteading. A loving and self-appointed protector, he guarded Sister Carmen physically in their travels, and she in turn imparted some of the Christian wisdom gleaned over many years of serving the Lord.

Jason anointed Sister Carmen with oil, and I prayed for her with my eyes closed. I was completely unprepared for what happened next. Sensing a pulling away by Jason, I cracked open my eyelids just in time to see him, frozen in position with his hands outstretched in ministering prayer, free-fall to the hard floor. So stunned that I failed to react, I watched as Jason hit the thin carpeting with a frighteningly loud *thump!* He lay there in an attitude of sleep while I stood, jaw unhinged and, a ridiculously helpless look on my face. Getting up a few minutes later, Jason said in hushed tones that he had witnessed Jesus overshadowing Sister Carmen.

At the time, I never doubted him, not for a moment. Despite hammering the floor with his head at concussion force he seemed unhurt, and he was so spiritual about the entire incident that I could barely speak.

Called to the Carpet

Anyone becoming involved with an active charismatic ministry knows what *being slain in the spirit* means by the end of his first week. It is so common in so many Pentecostal and charismatic services that if it fails to happen for a while, folks engaged in this practice begin to wonder why God's favor has left them. Experiencing the slain phenomenon for the first time at New Covenant, I have witnessed it probably hundreds of times in the past twelve years.

But what exactly does being slain in the spirit mean? Traditionally, the term applies to the supposed power of God coming upon a person at a specific time, overpowering his physical strength so that he or she is unable to stand. Sometimes while lying prone on the floor, the person is totally aware of the experience; at other times individuals claim that the power is so intense that all outside influences disappear. Visions are often seen during such trance-like states, or voices heard, usually attributed to God. Sometimes the person becomes stuck to the floor, as if held in place by an unseen hand. Some claim to have undergone tremendous spiritual renewal after "falling out," and still others claim physical healing.

During my years at New Covenant Fellowship I believed very strongly in the experience, recommended it to others, and marveled at the power of God that could cut a man's legs out from under him as with an invisible scythe. I have witnessed entire rows of people go down at the wave of a minister's hand, bodies collapsing in a disheveled heap on chairs or in the aisles. There were times the anointing seemed to come on me, and I was amazed that I'd lay hands on people or merely walk by them, and they would hit the floor with no warning.

The first time this happened, I was awed, deeply grateful that God's presence had manifested in such a powerful way through so inferior a vessel. I determined to walk more closely with Him, wanting to be used again in this way.

Carnality in Motion

At first, I was very caught up in the excitement, but in later years some disturbing hints began to surface that everything was not as I had first believed. For one thing, a few in our congregation seemed to swoon at the slightest hint of God's power in the room. Nancy Bullinger was one such, falling out more times than anyone else I knew. I thought it was because she was so sensitive to the things of the Spirit that God just naturally gravitated toward her to demonstrate His presence. But the closer I watched, the more nagging doubts tugged at me. On more than one occasion after she was supposed to be slain, I saw her sit up and pull her skirts down to a discreet level, the hem of which had risen inappropriately when she was laid on the floor by the catcher. She then lay back down and stayed there for a reasonably long period of time. This bothered me. If she was really under the power of God, as we believed, she would not have had the strength to move, much less be concerned about her modesty.

But this brought up another scriptural inconsistency. I Corinthians 14:40 addresses this concern: "Let all things be done decently and in order." Many of the women who had skirts or dresses fell with legs askew, exposing skin that should have, in decency, been covered. This obvious immodesty even spawned the *ministry of covering* in some churches, where specific individuals are assigned the duty of draping prepared cloths over the legs of women indecently exposed. One video of a Kenneth Hagin conference showed one of Hagin's aides going down to the floor under the power, falling into a sitting woman and sliding down the side of her legs—a woman, mind you, who was not his wife. This scenario was repeated in this video numerous times.[1]

Would the same God who commanded His people to do all things "decently and in order" also permit—rather instigate—a spiritual practice that places them in physically compromising positions?

Catch Me if You Can

In most services where being slain in the spirit occurs, some members of leadership are routinely assigned the duty of *catcher*. Their job is to stay behind the person being prayed for and be prepared to catch, should the individual be overcome, and to lay him gently on the floor while God "ministers." Since the job can be physically demanding, most of the catchers are men, and, since a great percentage of those slain are women, the catchers must come into abrupt physical contact with the woman's body. While a catcher is often able to lay hold of the woman's arms or shoulders, that is sometimes impossible. I have seen some women collapse so quickly and in such a free fall that the catcher has no time to consider appropriate contact, regardless of good intentions. Many people have swooned without prayer of any kind and with no warning beforehand. Those present are faced with the split-second choice of letting the person hit the floor with a thud or laying sudden hold on whatever limbs present themselves and lowering the person gently.

Sometimes they are not caught at all. There are simply too many at once responding to the power, and they fall one on top of another. During the early '90s I witnessed this aplenty, a mass of prone bodies sprawled out in the aisle, men on top of single women or other men's wives.

However you slice it, it comes up way short.

I had also been bothered by the very necessity for catchers. If God indeed was knocking His people down, surely He would have the mercy to cushion the fall. In all fairness, I have heard of some who were slain and hit the floor hard, but felt they landed on a bed of feathers. Jason had insisted he was unhurt after his falling out. But that, at best, is subjective. It may or may not have happened the way the person relates the experience. Embarrassment can be a strong silencing factor. Or there may be another reason for that altogether.

But people at times do get hurt, sometimes noticeably. I have personally seen at least one young man go down without realizing no catcher was behind him. He plummeted to the floor and cried out in obvious pain, holding his head. I wonder how many would fall down if they knew nobody would be there to lower them gently. A young church elder visiting our congregation from another town stood behind me as I received prayer during a Sunday service. Noticing I was shaking violently and fighting the urge to fall, he said quietly, "It's okay, I'm here. You won't get hurt."

Of course, I went down.

Context or Pretext?

Where does being slain in the spirit come from? The Bible, presumably. Our favored verse and the one uniformly lifted standard-like by the charismatic community is II Chronicles 5:13-14:

> It came even to pass, as the trumpeters and singers were as one, to make one sound to be heard in praising and thanking the LORD; and when they lifted up their voice with the trumpets and cymbals and instruments of musick, and praised the LORD, saying, For he is good; for his mercy endureth for ever: that then the house was filled with a cloud, even the house of the LORD;

> So that the priests could not stand to minister by reason of the cloud: for the glory of the LORD had filled the house of God.

Whenever anyone asked for scriptural proof for the validity of being slain in the spirit, we'd trot out this verse with a less-than-humble attitude. And, on the surface, it does look very similar to the modern practice.

There's just one small difficulty—that's not the end of the story.

Pastor Ted Brooks, in his devastating critique of modern false signs and wonders within the church, *I Was a Flakey Preacher*,[2] notes that we should continue to read down through chapters six and seven of II Chronicles, which is a continuation of this same narrative. Solomon addresses the multitudes present, prays to God, and way over in II Chronicles 7:1-2, we find a startling revelation:

Now when Solomon had made an end of praying, the fire came down from heaven, and consumed the burnt offering and the sacrifices; and the glory of the LORD filled the house.

And the priests could not enter into the house of the LORD, because the glory of the LORD had filled the LORD's house.

The priests were not able to minister in the house of God in the first place because they were not *in* the house of God at the time. They had come back out and stood with the large gathering of people after setting up the Ark of the Covenant in the holy place. While charismatic teaching would have us believe that the temple was littered with the bodies of incapacitated priests, the Old Testament simply tells us they could not even enter into the area where God had manifested His glory!

A quick reading of I Kings 8:10-11 will reveal the same thing. The priests simply were not in the holy place when it was filled with the glory of God.

We must look to Jesus. If He was the Word made flesh (John 1:14), then the entire canon of Scripture is summed up in Him. Not once is it even hinted at in Christ's ministry that being slain in the spirit ever occurred. It is true that when the soldiers came to take Him in the garden of Gethsemane, He spoke and they all "went backward, and fell to the ground" (John 18:6). But two things must be borne in mind here. For one thing, those who came to take Him were unbelievers and subject to His judgment. In this case, being slain in the spirit is not something to be sought after. Second, the mob didn't just stay on the ground for a while—they immediately got up again. If Christians are going to use this verse to support being slain in the spirit, it must be used in context with nothing withheld. Seen this way, this particular passage does more damage to the notion than provide support.

Daniel 10:9 has also been used with some success to validate the practice. Confronted by an angelic being, Daniel said "then was I in a deep sleep on my face, and my face toward the ground."

But again, one must read on to verses ten and eleven:

And, behold, an hand touched me, which set me upon my knees and upon the palms of my hands. And he said unto me, O Daniel, a man greatly beloved, understand the words that I speak unto thee, and stand upright: for unto thee am I now sent. And when he had spoken this word unto me, I stood trembling.

We need to take every word of God at face value. If Daniel says he fell into a deep sleep, we need to accept that without adding to or taking away. If some call this being slain in the spirit, another could as easily say that he simply passed out from fear. The contrasts between this and current practice are rather graphic. When Daniel was touched by the angelic messenger, he received strength to get up. In church when we were "touched by God," we lost strength. Daniel stood up to face the angel. We lay down so that God could *minister*. Daniel's encounter happened through no human agency, and without another witness present. Being slain in the spirit almost always happens under the touch or prayer of an anointed minister, and it is done in public. While it does happen on occasion when a Christian is alone or in prayer, these instances are reportedly rare, and again, subjective. I have seen enough instances, and experienced them myself, to recognize the effects of heightened expectation. The result is often just what the person believed would happen simply because the desire for the experience was so great.

A Visit With "God's Bartender"

This very thing happened to me in my living room with my wife and daughter present. When Rodney Howard-Browne and his new wine, get drunk anointing exploded onto the charismatic scene in the early '90s, both being slain in the spirit and *holy laughter* roared through our congregation, like wildfire. We grasped any teaching we could get on those subjects. With a five-pack of Rodney Howard-Browne videos, I sat down to glean as much as I could from this man. Since I hadn't the funds to travel to his itinerant services in Anchorage or Juneau, I reckoned this avenue the next best. I recall being disappointed with his preaching. Watching him maneuver through the congregation I couldn't see what all the fanfare was about. Mostly he told stories, anecdotes peppered with rehearsed jokes. He talked about the power and mocked those who questioned its origin. I struggled through the teaching because I wanted to get to the "glory." It was something dangled before me the entire time, and my expectations of being touched rose concurrent with my desire for the power. By the end of his teaching, I was primed, sitting on the edge of the couch.

When he spoke to the congregation and told them to expect the glory to manifest, I looked at Kris, who was combing my daughter Megan's hair. "I'm going to do it," I told her gravely, and stood.

I closed my eyes and listened to Browne's voice as he prayed. Suddenly, the decibel level shot through the roof.

"There it is!" he shouted, meaning the power of God. I listened as he described the anointing, which was supposed to be the manifest presence of God, as it moved up one side of the building and down the other, knocking people to the floor right and left.

When he shouted something like "Take it!" the air was forced out of me in a loud groan, and I fell like a rock back onto the couch. I heard Kris say of Megan, "Kev, you're scaring her."

But with my hands still raised and feeling "drunk in the spirit," I laughed, wept, and felt the power go all over my body, quite unconcerned about who was being frightened. It lasted maybe a half-hour, and when I came out of it I felt refreshed, a bit awed, and wanting more.

What happened there? An honest appraisal requires me to admit susceptibility to an emotional surge. It wasn't the power of God. I've seen this same form of manipulation in church services (my own included), whereby recipients are whipped into a fever pitch of expectation. Of course they will go down! That's what they've been waiting for throughout the entire service. It is only natural that they will respond at the appropriate time to the signals given by the man behind the pulpit.

My suspicions finally had an outworking about two years prior to my leaving New Covenant. By that time, having seen so much obvious hype, fakery, and emotionalism, I decided that if God was ever going to knock me down again, then He would be able to do it with my eyes open and my feet planted solidly. Although maintaining a respectful attitude about the entire practice, I was adamant that I would not fall prey to emotional manipulation.

I was never again slain in the spirit.

Whose Anointing?

It is important to understand that all of what goes on in a slain in the spirit service, regarding the actual manifestation, is attributed to the *anointing* of God. Depending on which River preacher you ask, this anointing can mean power, the weight of glory, the presence of God, or all of the above. While the Bible does refer to an anointing (I John 2:27), it has in these days of sensual faith been contorted almost beyond recognition. And as with so much of hyper-charismatic experience, it has been placed in the realm of something that needs to be reached for, pursued, or worked up in order to be obtained.

Many of today's biggest superstars in the church have redefined the anointing in a way that brings the experience more into agreement with occult forces than biblical truth. Benny Hinn told of his touch received at the grave of Foursquare founder Aimee Semple McPherson.[3] The anointing rests on her bones, he believes, and he shook with the power emanating from her long-dead body. The idea is that visiting these certain graves will give a double-dose of anointing. There's the "Rambo" anointing of one major Laughing Revival evangelist,[4] and the "Braveheart" anointing of Toronto Blessing's Wes Campbell.[5] It doesn't seem to matter that both Rambo and Braveheart are the main characters of two R-rated movies of gore, mayhem, and foul language. Then there's Carol Arnott's "Sword of the Lord" anointing, that makes you shake, cry out, and jerk violently. The video of this specific women's conference was very revealing.[6] I watched in amazement as one of the ladies participating behind the pulpit hefted a huge Scottish broadsword and passed it over the gathering to the congregational accompaniment of wails, groans, and manifestations. This was like something out of ancient Celtic wizardry.

Another major problem in the error-stricken part of today's charismatic subculture is that some people, usually big-name ministers like Kenneth Hagin, Kenneth Copeland, Benny Hinn, or John Kilpatrick, are looked upon as being more anointed than others. This naturally presupposes the necessity of making a journey to wherever they happen to be ministering in order to be touched by them, and consequently, by God. It is universally recognized by River adherents that the impartation of power is passed from person-to-person via the laying on of hands, and that belief has provoked a virtual scramble among regular church members to get to the preacher that has "it." It was certainly common practice among New Covenant membership to gravitate toward the most anointed minister who happened to be preaching at our meetings. Long lines formed before the power or prophecy minister, even if there were others less prominent in the visiting ministerial team that might be standing around with nothing to do and no one to pray for after the service.

Today's River proponents believe also that God moves in particular geographical locations, hence the necessity to get wherever God happens to be in order to get a touch from Him. Places like Toronto and Pensacola have become neo-Medieval pilgrimage destinations, and in fact, people are encouraged to make the journey by many of the front-running River preachers and by their own pastors. And this despite Jesus' obvious counter to that line of thinking when He told the Samaritan woman that physical locations mattered little in the eyes of God (John 4:21). The Temple made of stones would become obsolete. No more yearly pilgrimage. As long as we worship in Spirit and truth, He will dwell with us and reward us accordingly (John 4:20-24).

A little common sense might help here. What about the poor or those in some far distant corner of our planet who simply believe Christ's Gospel without knowledge of or desire for the Toronto anointing? Does it leave them out in the cold, or have they missed a necessary move of God? Plus, the fact that so much merchandising inarguably goes on in the form of videos, tee shirts, cassette recordings of worship music, conference fees, skyrocketing pastors' salaries—ad infinitum—that this current movement bears more of a resemblance to the money changers in the Temple than the humble followers of Jesus.

The Biblical Anointing

So what, actually, is the anointing? In the Old Testament, it was used to signify the setting apart of an object or the ordaining of an individual for special service to God (Exodus 30:22-30). The anointing oil was specially prepared according to the command of God, and was not to be used for any other purpose or manufactured without regard to God's specific instructions (Exodus 30:31-33). Kings as well as priests were anointed (I Samuel 10:1, I Samuel 16:13). Elisha was also anointed prophet by Elijah (I Kings 19:16). The act of pouring out the oil on an individual was used to signify God's selection, authority, and empowerment for the position.

But with the coming of Jesus Christ, this form of anointing (signifying God's choice for a position) with oil passed away* and was replaced with the anointing by the Holy Spirit, who Himself has come to live in each believer, empowering us to follow Christ (II Corinthians 1:21-22). He also is the one who ministers the gifts of the Spirit within the congregation (Romans 12:6-8, I Corinthians 12 and 14, Ephesians 4:8-12), and who performs works of miracles (Galatians 3:5) among His people. He leads us into all the truth, and reveals to us the things of God (I John 2:20, 27). This entire series of Scriptures, and many others on the same subject, shows us that the scriptural anointing is completely different from what is practiced today within the hyper-charismatic circles in which I once participated.

The anointing is not a thing conveniently passed from person-to-person—like getting zapped by a current of electricity a la Rodney Howard-Browne or Benny Hinn. To say, as we so often did in New Covenant Fellowship, "the anointing is now present for healing," or prophecy, or whatever, is to replace the indwelling Spirit with a physical feeling, emotion, or experience, and to separate Him from His ministry.

This is exactly what is suggested by terms like "getting plugged into the power." What this kind of thinking promotes is exactly what we are seeing within the River camp, the idea that we need something

---

*There are two New Testament references (James 5:14, Mark 6:13) to anointing the sick with oil.

more than we already possess as believers in Christ. This is precisely the original temptation in the Garden of Eden. Just look in the third chapter of Genesis. The fact is, if the Holy Spirit resides in us (and He isn't going anywhere), then His power is there as well, to enable us to do what He wants us to do. Anything added to what God has already provided is a counterfeit. We don't need to get zapped, or experience extra-biblical manifestations in order to feel that we have arrived, or to earn inclusion into the mythical great end-times army of Dominion or Latter Rain doctrine.

Examine the Source

Is there ever a real power at work? I have thought about this one long and hard, because if we admit that there is a genuine supernatural power manifesting, then in light of both the Scriptures and the voluminous evidences of carnality, we must conclude it is a spirit other than the Holy Spirit. Again, if this is so, that can only mean that Christians have opened themselves up to seducing spirits come to lead believers away from the one true God. I have come to the conclusion—very cautiously—that at times a real supernatural power is at work. In both River meetings and at the Brownsville Revival, documented testimonies from church leadership have involved vivid descriptions of people lifted bodily by an unseen force and violently thrown across the room and up against walls. Our own Tom Smalley told of being witness to this in one of Howard-Browne's Anchorage meetings. He'd seen a man well over two hundred pounds thrown back across three rows of chairs at the touch of God's Bartender. This is scary stuff. And it doesn't match anything I've come across in my Bible about God's dealings among His faithful covenant people.

I have experienced only two incidents of being slain that felt like a genuine power outside of myself. One was in a local Assembly of God service. A visiting woman preacher laid hands on many who had come forward for prayer, and a mass of them went down. Then it was my turn. Though she never so much as touched me, I felt a numbness sweep over my body, and I fell. On the floor, I shook uncontrollably for about ten minutes. The other time involved a service in my own congregation, again with the aid of a visiting minister. My wife, sitting in one of the pews, described my body contorting backward at a severe angle when the power hit me. To me, they both seemed supernatural. Whether or not that was the case, I will leave for the Lord to decide. If they were indeed supernatural, I now question from which source of power they truly came.

But I have yet to know of anyone, myself included, who, because of being slain experienced a changed life characterized by a love for the truth and a knowledge of God in agreement with the Scriptures. In my experience, the exact opposite has happened. When folks get touched with this kind of power, they routinely become almost unteachable, preferring the experience to the Word of God. I can't relate how many times I've heard, "Well, maybe I can't find it in the Scriptures, but it happened to me, so it's real!"

That's a dangerous step to take. In my many years of involvement with the occult prior to salvation, I had numerous real encounters with the supernatural. Certainly they could not have originated with God, but I once believed some of them did, and to me that was all that mattered. My ears were closed to any protest from Christian friends. Such a stubborn mindset is a fertile seedbed for deception. From just such a people will spring up a world ruler who will lead many to everlasting destruction:

> For the mystery of iniquity doth already work: only he who now letteth will let, until he be taken out of the way. And then shall that Wicked be revealed, whom the Lord shall consume with the spirit of his mouth, and shall destroy with the brightness of his coming: Even him, whose coming is after the working of Satan with all power and signs and lying wonders, And with all deceivableness of unrighteousness in them that perish; because they received not the love of the truth, that they might be saved. (II Thessalonians 2:7-10)

CHAPTER 5

THE WORD OF THE LORD?

"On Thursday, June the 9th, I will rip the evil out of this world."

These words, spoken in 1994 by reverend John Hinkle of Christ Church in Los Angeles, were to become another one of those defining moments for me. As a light breaking into darkness, I would learn, this time, to pay close attention to the Word of God despite a spectacular utterance of man.

Wednesday night fellowship at Nancy Bullinger's house was always a lively family time. Begun with a potluck, it naturally progressed into a short time of worship in the tight confines of her living room—chairs askew, people scrunched down in various positions wherever they could find room, hands raised, speaking in tongues. Not infrequently, a prophecy came forth. Mostly it had to do with how God was pleased with us, or loved us, or protected us from the enemy—pretty generic. Then would come the teaching, on a variety of subjects.

By this time, Jason Klein had left for a new start in another community, and Tom Smalley had taken over the pastorate. We appeared to be flourishing. Gaining new members, increasing in the "flow" of the Holy Spirit and the manifestation of spiritual gifts, we had attained a "maturity" that was beguiling. To tell the truth, I personally looked forward more to Wednesday nights than Sunday mornings, as it was more informal and everyone had an opportunity to participate.

On this particular evening, a knot of people was gathered around the center of the room just prior to the service's beginning. Someone was holding what I recall to be the transcript of John Hinkle's prophecy. It was the object of intense conversation, and as I read it myself I became very alarmed. Hinkle, whom I had never heard of, spoke of an abrupt supernatural cataclysm that would result in a *cleansing* (Hinkle's term) of the earth. Hinkle prophesied that God Himself said He would cleanse out this world, and it would be fully accomplished on June 9, 1994.[1]

Hinkle spoke of God sending out the angels to gather up the tares from the wheat fields to be burned, and about the removing of one man from the other as told in Luke 17:34. He noted it was not the Second Coming of Christ, but a removal of evil itself from the face of the earth, including evil men.

I have to be honest—I was frightened. For all my bluster about being one of God's elect, and not ever having to suffer His wrath, this prophecy had me rattled. June 9th was only about a week away. If what Hinkle prophesied was true, and I was not totally right with God, I would be swept away in the cleansing along with all the other evildoers. Much of the charismatic world was taking Hinkle seriously. He had not only given his prophecy to his congregation, but was invited onto Paul Crouch's Trinity Broadcasting Network to proclaim it via television.

I stewed for a few days about the prophecy—and prayed. Just a day or two before the prophesied deadline, I believe God quietly spoke to me while in prayer.

"What do the Scriptures say?"

That stopped me cold. What did the Scriptures say? Hinkle had indeed quoted some passages, but I had been so busy worrying, I hadn't taken the time to look them up. When I did, my fears began to evaporate. The one consistent thread running through all the parables that Hinkle quoted was this: they were not references to a pre-Second Coming cleansing, but the very return of Christ! Jesus was plainly speaking about the end of the age. To take those Scriptures any other way would be to twist them completely into some foreign context.

With my fears melting away, I knew in my heart that Hinkle was wrong. There would be no *ripping the evil out of this world*. The destruction of evil would certainly come, but not without the return of our Lord Himself. Hinkle had prophesied falsely.

The next fellowship I attended at Nancy's house had been switched to the day of the cleansing, the very day of the prophecy deadline. But the cleansing was only briefly mentioned. I recall Nancy saying half-jokingly, "Well, I guess old John Hinkle was wrong."

After the service we all went home, the world still retaining its full complement of evil men, and we never again mentioned it.

I understand John Hinkle did. Speaking to a presumably stunned congregation the following Sunday, he declared firmly that yes, God did rip the evil out of this world. It was only a spiritual veil of evil, Hinkle said, but it definitely was removed.

I can only shake my head now in sadness. Fortunately for this prophet, such a spiritual event is difficult for others to judge.

Thus Saith ... Who?

Presumptive prophecy is one of the biggest problems facing the church today. Prophecy, by its very nature a directive from God, has the effect of moving sincere believers in a particular direction. If the much-touted "word of the Lord" movement is false, then it is also laminated with a religious, good-looking veneer. If a humble apology is publicized, it has a numbing effect on discernment; as long as leadership sometimes confesses inadequacy, coupled with a "yearning for the Lord," many Christians are quick to forgive and to adjust their thinking accordingly. That's what happens in the Toronto Blessing, with its so-called prophetic animal manifestations in Christians; these manifestations originally caused a furor but have gained gradual acceptance due to an innovative spin on the Scriptures.

The point is, anything and everything is prophecy these days. Want to give a sluggish series of meetings an added boost? Just have someone prophesy that God is in it and wants to bless everyone in attendance, and you'll fill every seat in the house. As far as accountability is concerned, there is basically none. If a prophecy proves embarrassingly false, those involved just don't talk about it. The people seldom ask questions and will forget the failed prophecy in a very little while. I know—I've seen it repeated more times than I can remember. One of our members was prophesied over by a visiting preacher that he would have a tremendous healing ministry. However, he died two years later without the pronouncement being fulfilled and only a brief mention of it, lacking sufficient explanation, was heard from the pulpit. To the best of my remembrance, no one ever called it a false prophecy.

We have failed miserably to hold to the clear guidance of Scripture:

> And if thou say in thine heart, How shall we know the word which the LORD hath not spoken? When a prophet speaketh in the name of the LORD, if the thing follow not, nor come to pass, that is the thing which the LORD hath not spoken, but the prophet hath spoken it presumptuously: thou shalt not be afraid of him. (Deuteronomy 18:21-22)

Now look at verse 20 and think about it for a moment:

> But the prophet, which shall presume to speak a word in my name, which I have not commanded him to speak, or that shall speak in the name of other gods, even that prophet shall die.

Presumption (i.e., false prophecy) was punishable by death! God said this. Speaking in the name of the Lord is serious business with God because if a prophet spoke from his own heart or was listening to deceiving spirits, he could easily lead astray an entire nation. And that's exactly what happened in the days of Isaiah, Jeremiah, and Ezekiel:

> A wonderful [appalling*] and horrible thing is committed in the land; The prophets prophesy falsely, and the priests bear rule by their means; and my people love to have it so: and what will ye do in the end thereof? (Jeremiah 5:30-31)

---

*The Hebrew meaning from the Strong's Concordance.

Ponder these words—appalling, horrible, falsely, and finally, love. The Israelites had become so enamored of honeyed words falling from the mouths of those who styled themselves God's spokesmen that when the truth finally came forward in the person of Jeremiah, they sought to kill him. Why does God take false prophecy so seriously? Because it always dishonors His name and leads the people to worship a false image rather than the true God.

Pleasant Words

One of the biggest problems evident in our congregation was the fact that so few prophecies were corrective. I do not remember one of them specifically address the heretical teachings we had so hungrily devoured over the years. Surely God has not changed His tactics with His covenant people. The coming of Christ did not invalidate His hatred for the false, or His hard dealing with those who preached it. One of the main ministries of a true prophet of God was to confront and publicly expose those who spoke falsely in the name of the Lord. You see it happening repeatedly in Scripture. It is not a pleasant duty, and it brought swift and at least verbally violent antagonism onto the head of the true prophet from those who opposed the Lord's Word. But correction was something that simply had to be done if the Lord's covenant people were to be taught the difference between the truth and the lie, the holy and the profane. And, as the Bible makes very plain, everyone who speaks falsely and with impunity in the name of the Lord will be brought to judgment.

Tom Smalley often noted with satisfaction that not *one* of the visiting ministers, prophets, or anointed circuit-riding overseers of our flock ever rebuked or corrected us for false doctrine. In fact, he said, it was quite the contrary. Tom said repeatedly that these ministries commended our group as loving, doctrinally solid, and thriving—i.e. biblical. This is interesting in the light of a true prophet's credentials. In Scripture, the validity of any prophetic office was directly proportional to its exposure of false teaching.

This brings to mind the words of the prophet Isaiah and his open rebuke of apostate Israel:

> That this is a rebellious people, lying children, children
> that will not hear the law of the LORD: Which say to the
> seers, See not; and to the prophets, Prophesy not unto us
> right things, speak unto us smooth things, prophesy deceits.
> (Isaiah 30:9-10)

Although very painful, cleaning out an infected wound is absolutely necessary, or the limb will turn gangrenous. Further neglect will result in the death of the whole person. The truth hurts. It divides asunder, and lays bare what we would rather have remain unnoticed. Faithfulness to the God who redeemed us demands submission to His loving discipline (Hebrews 12:5-6).

The biblical mandate is for purity of doctrine. I seriously question any ministry that is unable or unwilling to discern and confront that which is in direct opposition to the Word of God. The ministries who complemented ours were in agreement with New Covenant's own teachings and practices; to rebuke or correct our leadership would have resulted in their own admission of guilt.

The Face in the Mirror

While we at New Covenant knew that false prophets and heretical teachers were somewhere out there, we never understood that they would be right in our midst, within our church itself. While perhaps not qualifying as wolves preying on the flock, many of us nonetheless taught many extra-biblical things, contrary to the Scriptures. For all our sermonizing about strong adherence to the Word, we very often set Scripture aside when our prophecies didn't match "that which is written." Teaching on false prophecy or false shepherds stood near absolute zero, and certainly none were named. If one in our midst would dare question a prized minister whose teachings we imbibed, he was routinely made to feel spiritually immature and lacking in understanding. I bore the brunt of this demeaning attitude on some occasions, and at other times I was guilty of administering it. Our leadership wanted the blessings but not the warnings. But what do Paul and Peter have to say?:

For I know this, that after my departing shall grievous wolves
enter in among you, not sparing the flock. Also of your own
selves shall men arise, speaking perverse things, to draw away
disciples after them. Therefore watch, and remember, that
by the space of three years I ceased not to warn every one
night and day with tears. (Acts 20:29-31)

But there were false prophets also among the people, even as
there shall be false teachers among you, who privily shall bring
in damnable heresies, even denying the Lord that bought them,
and bring upon themselves swift destruction. (II Peter 2:1)

One in our congregation, heavily into the prophetic movement,
once stood and gave a revelation from the Lord. Speaking on Matthew
12:36, where Jesus stated that people would be called to account for
every idle word spoken, she said God had shown her we would not
be condemned for careless utterances, only deprived of gifts for not
speaking good ones. Checking my Bible right then, I exchanged a concerned glance with Kris. The error of this sister's declaration became
immediately evident. Verse 37 of Matthew 12 clearly states: "For by thy
words thou shalt be justified, and by thy words thou shalt be *condemned*"
(emphasis mine). Jesus could not have been the author of this sister's
revelation because His own words in Scripture contradicted hers. By
that time, I was already in hot water with the leadership for openly
discussing my doubts about some things, so I kept quiet. No one else
in the room seemed to notice any discrepancy.

While it was all very well and good to warn our flock of the danger
of cults such as Mormonism, we neglected to bring the mirror of
truth to our own face. Self-examination was critical for the health of
our congregation, but when it came to false doctrine, in this area we
habitually looked the other way.

The Measuring Rod

The Scriptures tell us that to question someone bringing in strange
doctrine is not immature but wise. And how do you know the

difference? You know it when the Jesus they bring will not match up with Jesus as He revealed Himself in Scripture (II Corinthians 11:4). For years, I sensed something was not quite right. Often, the word being preached did not bring life. I went to Sunday worship hungry to be fed, anxious for spiritual food, and ten minutes into the service would be nearly overcome with boredom and desperately wanting to leave, but fearing that something was wrong with *me*. Returning home later, I would be heavy with depression, believing I had failed God—again. The next Sunday would duplicate the previous one.

Many things we were taught just didn't add up. For instance, although the Old Testament prophets were supposed to be right one hundred percent of the time, Christians "moving" in the gift of prophecy, or even those filling the "prophetic office" didn't have to line up with that precise margin of accountability—or so we were told. The reasoning went that although God moved in judgment during the days of Isaiah, for Christians He now gives tremendous grace, offering them lots of time to "grow into" the prophetic and to finally one day "mature." All this, despite the fact there is not one recorded instance of false prophecy among New Testament prophets.

Another issue concerning this maturing process is that, if a prophet needs to mature in his gifting, then so do all the other believers listed in I Corinthians 12. An institution called the "School of the Prophets" is gaining credence in the church, and springing up in various forms nationwide. At New Covenant this classroom forum was spoken of highly as an avenue to tutor developing prophets into maturity. Literally anyone who felt in themselves a prophetic leaning would qualify for this personal prophetic education. I'm curious how a person can mature in the working of miracles, or the gifts of healing, or the discerning of spirits. How do you mature in signs and wonders? The point is, prophecy is a supernatural act, an empowering of the Holy Spirit, the same as miracles (I Corinthians 12:4-6). If a prophet can only learn to prophesy correctly in increments, then it makes sense that a worker of miracles would likewise be limited as to his initial power in ministry. Tongue in cheek, let's consider a hypothetical event. Suppose a Christian, suddenly empowered by God, were to multiply bread for a huge crowd, as Jesus did (John 6:1-13).

But instead of having baskets of food left over, this novice comes up a few loaves short. Using the same logic some apply to present-day prophets, we'd have to say he needed to "grow into his ministry" a bit more, in order to fully be able to work miracles properly.

Get the idea? We have applied two different standards to what should be the same supernatural working of God in both the prophetic and the working of miracles. This is not scriptural. We need to adhere to the one or the other—either make everything subjective and based upon our individual feelings and beliefs or adhere to the unmoving standard the Word of God delivered once for all to the saints (I Kings 18:21).

Biblical Hall of Fame

At New Covenant, our Wednesday home meetings were always ripe for prophecy of any kind, which almost always fell into the "bless me" category. Usually a few, recognized within our congregation as prophetic, would speak out what they believed to be the oracles of God. Personal prophecy was not merely accepted but sought after, and a really good fellowship time featured a "word" of encouragement or direction coming from the Lord. One such service featured Pastor Tom laying hands on about six or seven of us, one at a time, and proclaiming various biblical names over us, indicating the particular anointing in our lives. I was Samuel, a shepherd of the people during a time of spiritual drought. It was spoken that I had a pastor's heart for the flock, etc. Nancy became Dorcas, due to her frequent generosity and reaching out to the needy in the church, and so on.

May I say, without malice, that nothing prophetic was needed for these proclamations. Literally *anyone* in our group knew by watching us what our specific leanings were. It did not require a "word from the Lord" to identify it. I have to admit that being named Samuel that night stuck with me for a long time, stroking my pride and comforting me during times I was uncertain about my relationship with Christ. I figured if *God* called me Samuel, then He surely had His hand of approval on me.

Absentee Fathers

During an October 1997 church seminar, a prophecy was given over Tom that he would have a back country ministry extending into portions of the Canadian Northwest. It was recorded on my cassette copy of that seminar that many, many would stand in heaven due to his preaching the Word as a circuit rider, or traveling minister. While he did minister to a couple of smaller church groups in a portion of the prophesied area a time or two, he left for the east coast less than two years after that prophecy was proclaimed.

Also, during the time when "spiritual headship" was again beginning to gain popularity (it has become even more so since I left New Covenant), Tom was called "father" of our town by some in prophetic ministry, and he was told "by the word of the Lord" that he no longer needed to ask for opinion or input on certain subjects. He was to walk in this authority because, he was told, he had earned it. Can you understand what this kind of word spoken over an individual is capable of doing to his spiritual equilibrium? When someone is told he no longer needs to seek counsel in certain decisions because God has already given him the authority to act, the result is disastrous.

It should be relatively easy to discern the source of these prophecies. Do we *earn* a place of ministry, or, as Paul states in his self-effacing way, do we humbly acknowledge that "[B]y the grace of God I am what I am" (I Corinthians 15:10)? Can we ever reach a point in our ministry that we no longer need to ask the counsel of godly brothers and sisters in a specific area of our lives? And finally, does God bless absentee fathers? If that were a true word of the Lord for Tom, it would seem he would have been told by God to stay put and fulfill his ministry.

When I questioned him about these prophecies after learning of his upcoming move, I was met with a shrug of the shoulders and no explanation whatever.

Pieces of the Puzzle

After taking over the pastorate from Jason, Tom would often say from the pulpit, "There is a tremendous anointing for the prophetic in this church." Echoing ministers who visited our congregation, this meant that a high percentage of prophetic people were in our membership. Often, especially during a Sunday service, a few people would contribute to form a single prophecy. Someone would offer a portion, then another would pick it up and so on, until the prophecy was "complete." The Scripture used to justify this, "For we know in part, and we prophesy in part" (I Corinthians 13:9). But this verse, when looked at in its proper context, has nothing to do with prophesying incrementally. The passage simply indicates that, until Christ returns, we will not understand the whole picture. But the verse was used to rationalize a process that finds no support in the Word of God.

Tom held the prophetic in the highest esteem, especially when it came from a barrage of high-powered prophets within the ranks of the River. He considered himself a prophet on the order of I Corinthians 14 and, in his own words, possibly even attaining to the office of a prophet according to Ephesians 4:11. He had been validated as such by various ministers who came through the area and preached at New Covenant. He was a voracious reader of books by prophetic authors, he watched videos of prophetic ministers (sometimes entire home fellowship times were dedicated to such viewings), and he often invited itinerant or circuit ministers with a "prophetic anointing."

Interestingly, although Tom's prophetic office and function was the basis of so much at New Covenant, he himself often had a difficult time getting it right. Our congregation once met in the basement of a large community building, whose upstairs auditorium held a seating capacity of three hundred. We'd frequently hear Tom say to the congregation that God showed him one day every seat would be filled. Yet, as of this writing, New Covenant's membership has dwindled dramatically. Plus, I've lost count of the times he took the pulpit, announced he had fully prepared a message for that Sunday's service, and God changed it on him "at the last minute." It should be logically obvious that at least *one* of the two messages Tom prepared was not from God. But, characteristically, nobody said a thing.

All these instances were puzzle pieces shaped like red flags, warning that we had strayed from God's way.

(Common) Sense

Often in the ministry time following the official close of the service, people would gather for prayer and encouragement. When we had visiting speakers who were noted for prophetic ministry, it was normal practice for our members to receive from them the laying on of hands with an accompanying prophetic word. Listening to tape recordings of these services, my memory is refreshed concerning telling phrases that popped up with predictable regularity. "I'm sensing right now," or "I'm sensing by the Spirit" was often spoken by the prophets over individuals in our flock. While on the surface it may seem unimportant, a closer look in a biblical context might give us pause.

What these phrases really mean is, "I feel," or "I have an impression." Considering all the trouble my feelings have gotten me into regarding doctrine and practice, I'd slam on the brakes should anyone speak to me like that now. Biblically documented prophecy cannot in any way be compared to this kind of practice. The prophetic word given by God's spokesmen for both individuals and nations was strong, sure, and unhesitating in both the Old and New Testament. In Scripture, prophecy is never exploratory. God knows what He wants to say to people and is quite capable of making sure those He's chosen to deliver the message will get it right the first time.

When David was in sin with Bathsheba, the prophet Nathan confronted him head-on and declared, "Thou art the man" (II Samuel 12:7). When a prophet was moved by the Holy Spirit, what came forth from him was a pure direction, correction, or accusation from God. New Testament prophecy, we are told by today's prophetic elite, is not quite so exacting, especially in the corporate setting. I Corinthians 14:24-25, tells an entirely different story:

> But if all prophesy, and there come in one that believeth not, or one unlearned, he is convinced of all, he is judged of all: And thus are the secrets of his heart made manifest; and so falling down on his face he will worship God, and report that God is in you of a truth.

Doesn't sound like a hesitant ministry to me.

Riding Shotgun

While much of today's prophetic movement appears powerful and exhilarating, the recipient of such ministry can often find himself wrapped in a deceptive fog. All the prophetic services I attended through New Covenant, and those I've watched on television, have left me wanting. To the discerning listener, the prophetic word for a variety of individuals sounds remarkably similar. How many times I've heard prophesied over others and myself that, "God has heard the cry of your heart. He is drawing you to Himself to accomplish a great work, one that will reach far past anything your mind is able to conceive. He has given you a heart of compassion for others, and He has seen the brokenness in your life. All the pain you've endured these past seasons you've not suffered alone. God has been with you through it all, and He is raising you up to do a mighty work for Him and His kingdom."

Well, to an insecure person or one who runs from one prophetic conference to another in search of a spiritual high, the above prophecy sounds great. "Whew!" you think. "God really has seen my hurts this past year, and He has been with me all the times I felt so alone. God is mending my broken heart, and now He's about ready to bring me into the place where I can do tremendous things for His kingdom."

May I say, again without malice or sarcasm—anyone can learn those very things just by reading the Bible. God says them over and over in the pages of Scripture, just so we will know His promises. And yes, He has called us to a great work, even if that work is being a faithful housewife or janitor who will shine with His love.

The above is what is known as a shotgun prophecy. It applies to virtually anyone at any time. Like a blast from a good twelve gauge, it scatters so many generic words that some of them are bound to hit the target, no matter who you are.

How often have you heard that, "the enemy has come against you and God will rout him?"

Well, of course! The enemy (Satan) has come against every single one of God's covenant people since the dawn of time, and will continue to do so until his final destruction in the lake of fire. And God will rout our demonic foes if we abide faithful to Him.

The Hidden Things of God?

As Jason Klein was heavily involved in this arena, it was only natural that Tom should assume the role of his mentor. Sometimes however, the prophetic was only for the super-spiritual, taking on the esoteric qualities inherent in a master/disciple relationship of the highest and most secret order. Kris and I discovered this early in our years at New Covenant. We had been invited to Jason's house for dinner one evening, a year or so before he left the congregation for points north. I don't recall what initiated the conversation, but Jason became agitated about the inability of certain people to grow into what was always referred to as "the deep things of God." He stated that he had written out a complete and lengthy prophecy given him by the Lord, but its contents were so intense that no one would be able to rightfully assess and apply the teachings therein. He said almost angrily, "If some people read it [the prophecy], they'd say, 'God couldn't say that!' Oh yeah? God can say whatever He wants."

That's simply not true. God will never speak or do anything contrary to His character or His written Word, the Bible. Jesus was the Word made flesh. All that God wanted us to know about Himself is revealed in His Son, and recorded in the only reliable written testimony of the Godhead. But the ultra-sovereignty doctrine making headway these days allows God the elbow room to do just about anything. Some see Him making His people act like eagles and bulls in church services. On his March 29, 2000 broadcast of *This Is Your Day*, Benny Hinn bragged that someone prophesied Jesus would physically appear on stage with Hinn. Although the actual prophecy came forth from Ruth Heflin of gold dust fame, Hinn raved about the word and looked forward to its fulfillment at not just one, but many of his crusades.

It doesn't take a Bible scholar to see that Christ forewarned about this very thing:

Wherefore if they shall say unto you, Behold, he is in the desert; go not forth: behold, he is in the secret chambers; believe it not. For as the lightning cometh out of the east, and shineth even unto the west; so shall also the coming of the Son of man be. (Matthew 24:26-27)

Rick Joyner is another seer who has had great impact on the Christian prophecy scene. For years a favorite among those of my former congregation, his book, *The Final Quest*, took our leadership by storm. Along with other prophets, Joyner was also spotlighted via video in home groups led by Tom Smalley. Joyner's blatant Latter Rain beliefs were assimilated into our congregation on the wings of the mythical end-times revival which would supposedly sweep millions into the kingdom. A super-spiritual elite group of prophets and apostles will be raised up, Joyner states, and will transform the world of these last days, doing greater miracles than even the apostles who walked with our Lord. Whole nations will tremble at the mention of their names.

Interesting. Sounds a lot easier to deal with than Jesus' prophecy that "[Y]e shall be hated of all nations for my name's sake" (Matthew 24:9).

In Joyner's book, the spirit of a deceased saint, who claims to be one of the foolish virgins, equates outer darkness with a passing punishment after death.[2] In confusing the two parables of the ten virgins and the unfaithful steward with the talents, this supposed departed believer tells Joyner that the outer darkness is only temporary, a grieving experience upon death for a wasted life on earth. This claim is astounding, and it warrants close examination:

First, even if *Joyner* had forgotten the context of our Lord's parables (both of which are found back to back in Matthew 25), this spirit, if he were of the heavenly sort, would never have done so. It is the unfaithful steward in the parable of the talents, not the foolish virgins, who gnashed his teeth in outer darkness. Any spirit confusing the two could not have been a heavenly being. Second, the outer darkness with its "weeping and gnashing of teeth" is *never* mentioned in the context of a passing experience. Rather, it is always biblically portrayed as an eternal state of being. Every time the term outer darkness is used by Jesus it is in reference to hell, the everlasting flames of punishment for sins committed while on earth. (See Matthew 8:12, 13:42, 13:50, 22:13, 24:51, 25:30, and Luke 13:27-28.) The entire context of Matthew 25 is an everlasting separation between the faithful and the unfaithful, and the reward or punishment appointed.

Say what you will, hell (the outer darkness) is not temporary.

For any spirit to contradict such a plain scriptural truth exposes its origins as either the mind of man or the realm of the demonic. Besides, having contact with the dead is occultic and flatly forbidden in Scripture (Deuteronomy 18: 10-12). Clearly, God would not send the spirit of a deceased saint to talk with Rick Joyner in his vision when the very practice itself is forbidden by God.

Prophecy on Demand

Listening to some of the tape recordings of our meetings, it strikes me that often a word was something to be asked for by leadership and that God would obligingly provide. I've often been in leadership meetings when a visiting overseer would be asked if God had a word for the individual elders and their wives. The prophet usually complied, and his seeking the Lord on the matter would be rewarded in seconds with a revelatory directive that each person certainly took to heart. The man administering these prophecies is a very nice man, loving and considerate, and a church planter abroad. Although I personally like him, in retrospect I can't help feeling he'd been repeatedly put on the spot and was expected to perform. Considering that so many of his utterances went unfulfilled or turned out just the opposite, the source of his words at those times seems self-evident.

Donations or Death

I well recall one famous televangelist's 1987 plea to fund a certain portion of his ministry. Speaking nationwide, he said that God told him that if the money wasn't raised, God would take this man home. In other words, this minister would die. When I heard about it, I became confused because I genuinely liked the guy. I had listened to him preach, read his books, and agreed with his material. But this one really bothered me. Would God take the man's life on account of a financial deficit? Kicking into rationalization mode, I figured that if it did happen, it was because God didn't deem the world worthy of a man of his caliber. After all, if God's own people didn't provide the funds to keep this man's ministry empire going, then they deserved neither the man nor the facilities.

The money was raised, some eight million dollars, I believe, and this minister's life was spared.

Of course, I believe far differently now. God didn't threaten Oral Roberts' life. For one thing, God doesn't hold His people for ransom. When I finally began to raise some disturbing questions among our leadership, I was told Brother Oral simply made a mistake. I would correct this notion—five dollars is a mistake, eight million is a travesty. But it just goes to demonstrate the bizarre lengths to which some will go in order to justify reprehensible actions within their own ranks.

Despite the obvious implications of the Oral Roberts millions-of-dollars affair, at least one of our young people from New Covenant attended Oral Roberts University and received commendation for doing so. When she returned to Alaska for summer vacation she was offered a few minutes pulpit time to give us a report on her progress. Among other things, she noted that "the fullness of the Godhead dwells in us." While she hadn't gotten that quote from Oral Roberts (she named another famous healing evangelist), no one bothered to correct her.

A Cloth of Blended Fabric

Over and over I have heard the refrain, "Well, I know he's off in some areas, but he teaches some really good stuff, too. We just need to chew the meat and spit out the bones."

Just where is this line of reasoning found in Scripture? Salt and fresh water do not ever flow from the same source (James 3:11-12). In sermons, Tom Smalley would often remind us of the mixture of flesh and spirit we should actually expect in prophecy ("that's just the way it is"), despite the fact that Scripture states emphatically that God hates mixture:

> Ye shall keep my statutes. Thou shalt not let thy cattle gender with a diverse kind: thou shalt not sow thy field with mingled seed: neither shall a garment mingled of linen and woollen come upon thee. (Leviticus 19:19)

The point of this passage is not really about mixing cottons and synthetics in our daily attire. The whole of the chapter speaks of doing things God's way, and not copying the attitudes of the world around us and mixing them into our relationship with Him.

With prophecy, a simple failure in judgment can be corrected, a sin can be forgiven, but one glaring error right after another disqualifies a person for ministry. Until he gets his own house in order, such a believer needs to refrain from instructing others (Romans 2:21). While we are exhorted in I Thessalonians 5:20 not to despise prophecy, as it is a bona fide gift of the Holy Spirit, we must heed the admonition of the following verse to carefully and with godly judgment examine what comes forth in the midst of the Christian assembly and hold fast only to that which measures up to scriptural standards. If it came to my attention that my banker handled funds the way some in the Christian prophecy market manipulate the Word of God, I would immediately close my entire account.

If we demand strict accountability in such perishable things as money, how much more should we expect in spiritual matters.

Examining the Evidence

It is with a heavy sigh and great sadness that I look back on those days. We'd make such a big issue about how important the Scriptures were to us, but just let one of us confront a favored doctrine in someone's life and the response was invariably negative. Often, if I disagreed with a certain big-name teacher's doctrine, Tom would strongly recommend a book for me to read, with the suggestion it would help me to mature in order to accept the things being promoted within our group. But again, I didn't want to read a book—I wanted to go to the Bible! Yet it never was accepted practice to critically assay teachings in the light of the Scriptures. Not once in the dozen years Kris and I attended our former group did leadership stop the teaching, turn off the video, or pull the plug on the television (Trinity Broadcasting Network, Benny Hinn, et al.), open the Bible and carefully examine what we were being taught. The very opposite was in force.

About five years prior to our leaving, I had read in secret a book by Dave Hunt and T. A. McMahon titled *The Seduction of Christianity*.[3] (Why should a Christian be so afraid of church leadership that he feels he has to read contradictory evidence in secret?) The book detailed an amazing amount of deception entering the church via New Age sources. With direct quotes and voluminous documentation of aberrant teachings from Kenneth Copeland, Earl Paulk, and a veritable who's who in today's charismatic movement, the writing duo critically outlined the assault on biblical truth and the shift away from the Scriptures to the realm of feelings and experiences. I was stunned and shaken and so alarmed, I told Kris what I had read. Curious about Pastor Tom's reaction to the book, she broached the subject at the mid-week fellowship at Nancy's house (which I did not attend). Tom's response floored her:

"Yes," he retorted, suddenly angry, "I've heard about that book, and it splits churches! I won't even read it!"

Flaring up silently, Kris left the house and came home fuming. Tom did show up later that evening and apologized for his reaction, but not for his stance. He hadn't read the book, yet he judged its contents flawed. Why? Because it touched on people in the charismatic field, people whose books Tom had read, whose doctrines he had absorbed. As it was then, it is now. I have had the same basic reaction from others since beginning my own doctrinal research several years ago.

Do we so cling to our individual preferences that we refuse to weigh legitimate concerns about doctrines that contradict God's Word? Sadly, we seem to have reached that point. It took a year of pleading before I could get a hearing before the eldership regarding the false doctrines within our own group. Two meetings resolved the issue—in the eyes of the leadership. They felt no need to formally discuss it again and moved on to more mundane church business. This attitude is rife within the charismatic arena. People willingly close their ears to something they just don't want to hear.

CHAPTER 6

EVERY WIND OF DOCTRINE

"I see this place as a training center."

Jason Klein vacated the pastorate sometime around 1990 or 1991, transferring authority to Tom Smalley just prior to his departure. The training center was Jason's idea at first, and he spoke of it often. He originally envisioned a complex of discipleship tutoring and vocational instruction with on-site workshops. He passed the idea along to Tom, who eagerly received it and attempted to outline the method by which the plan would be implemented. With an eye toward the future, both in building sites and community resources, Tom led the way into the theological grounding that would precede any physical structures erected by our church group.

And that meant books—lots of them—along with videos, classes, home group meetings, pulpit teachings, and despite our loathing of the word because it sounded so *religious*, even programs. It is impossible to tally every teaching in which we immersed ourselves. There were simply too many. Nobody could ever accuse our congregation of being a stagnant church, as we always pursued one theological fad after another with the speed of a voracious consumer.

"Cutting a Covenant"

The book (and class) *Covenant Relationships* taught the meaning of the Old Testament covenant between God and Abraham, then progressed into the New Testament era between Christ and the church.[1] While there may have been some good points made in the book, as always our congregation took it to impractical extremes. Class attendance was heavily promoted, and absence publicly frowned upon. This was the first time I heard the term, "cut a covenant." I never found it per se in the Bible, but as a unit of understanding, the term was incredibly popular. Instructed to realize our covenant relationship not only with Christ but also with one another, intimate bonding with all members of our group was strongly encouraged.

This was simply not possible, since there are only an allotted portion of hours in a given day. Although Christian fellowship includes deep friendships, it also includes mere acquaintances and persons of varying degrees of church participation, not all of whom wish to be relationally close. To attempt to develop and maintain an intimacy with every member of our congregation would have precluded nearly every other facet of the average day, including the daily eight hours of work most of us had.

Biblically, we as Christians do not need to establish a covenant with one another. That was an Old Testament institution used by both Israelites and pagans for mutual protection, establishing friendships, and a variety of other purposes. When God used the model of covenant between Himself and Israel, He required circumcision of the Hebrew males in order for them to be included. In Christ, circumcision is of the heart (Romans 2:29), and anyone who believes in Him is already included in covenant relationship. We cannot covenant with each other because Christ has already done it for us. This mindset of covenant precipitated what I can only view as a falling back under the Law. During one Sunday service, Tom declared openly that he would never again shave his beard, as an outward sign of a covenant he made with God. This was clearly a human effort on Tom's part. To attempt a covenant symbol of our own making is dangerous and contrary to the Scriptures.

The question that arises from the example of Tom's vow is: would shaving the beard indicate a severing of the covenant between Tom and Christ? The answer of course would be no. And what if Tom changed his mind, shaved, and everyone noticed it? If not dealt with scripturally, the person who vowed is swamped by guilt and/or embarrassment for not keeping an unnecessary public commitment between himself and God—which was by his own initiation.

On the Wings of Angels

Some books brought into our midst, although generally kept in the background, added to our tremendous doctrinal confusion. In a leadership meeting Tom spoke to us about the guardian angels assigned to us. These angelic beings, he said, have been given the task of guiding us into the knowledge of the Gospel. From the time of our birth our angel would continue to lead us, all the way to the day of our deaths. If we rejected the message of Christ each time it was presented, the angel was instructed to start all over again and bring us to salvation in Christ.

Although I did not openly question it, I wondered where in the Bible I could locate such a teaching. It goes without saying that it is not there at all. In fact, it sounds identical to the teachings in a book called *Angels On Assignment* written by Charles and Frances Hunter, as told to them by Pastor Roland Buck.[2] The volume chronicles the *spiritual* exploits of Pastor Buck. He claimed to have been visited by the angel Gabriel, played host to squadrons of warrior angels in his home, watched as they petted and played with his dog, and was eventually taken to stand before God in heaven. The "Lord" even gave Buck a parchment to take back to earth. It conveniently turned to ashes shortly after his return to terra firma.

Due to its repeated violation of the scriptural record, the book has been long discredited by a variety of respected ministries. It nonetheless continues to enjoy popularity among some charismatics.

This book had been in the New Covenant Fellowship office for years, and since Tom's own teaching was a mirror image, I can only assume that's where he got the idea. Personalized angelic protection certainly resonated with the barrage of like teachings that catered to our self-importance and unbiblical fascination with spiritual beings.

The (Not So) Healthy Body

Cell groups became a number one priority for an extended period. The concept is taken from the human cell, which reproduces healthy counterparts if it has the proper nutrients. While home group meetings should be a welcome addition to the life of a local congregation, our particular brand of meeting, carried out in several homes, involved spiritual warfare of the "bringing down principalities and powers in high places" genre, casting demons out of Christians, and such unbiblical doctrines as *soul ties*. The idea behind the soul tie is a mystical connection between flesh and spirit, such as supposedly occurs when adultery is committed. Until the soul tie is broken, the teaching goes, the partners will continue to be sexually attracted to each other and will be united in a way that can only be severed by prayer and renunciation. It is basically spiritual warfare on a personal level.

The soul ties doctrine and its attendant practice were highlighted in one of our Sunday meetings by a visiting prophet who made routine stops at New Covenant. His text that Sunday morning came from Judges 19, where a man took his dead concubine and cut her into twelve pieces, then sent the individual body parts to the various tribes in Israel. The minister spiritualized this act and preached on soul ties, and how each dismembered piece represented a part of a person's life connected to another, or to many others, by the sexual act. Noting it was necessary to break off these ties, he called forward any who had led promiscuous lives prior to conversion, that they might be free and whole. Several responded, and the service was viewed by leadership as a great success.

Again, this particular doctrine is found nowhere in Scripture, but was used liberally in our congregation to explain certain repetitive behavior. Interestingly, what we termed soul ties, the Bible has always called lusts (I Peter 2:11). We don't need to slice through any ethereal umbilical cord binding us to another. Such theology finds it roots in New Age thought.

The Pied Piper

The Final Quest, by Rick Joyner, took center stage in one of our home groups. It was introduced into our congregation, through video, by former pastor Jason Klein. This is so ironic, because though living in a far northern community, his pastoral reach still extended to New Covenant Fellowship. The film, shot in Jason's living room with him sitting on the couch and facing the camera, was an hour-long presentation of his spiritual self-discovery, his apologies to the congregation for any harm he may have brought, and a glowing appraisal of *The Final Quest*, which he believed held the key to understanding the last days' struggle of the church against the forces of Satan. It is interesting in retrospect to note that Jason's apologies never included having introduced false doctrine via Copeland, Hagin, being slain in the spirit, or the spiritual warfare nonsense.

Having gathered most of the leadership to watch the video, then-pastor Tom Smalley appeared genuinely impressed. Some of us were a bit less enthusiastic. Kris thought Jason was grandstanding and privately told me so. As for myself, the content of Rick Joyner's book is what most alarmed me. Jason mentioned an incident where the spirit of a man Joyner had known on earth allegedly communicated with him. The spirit stated that he had to repent of sins *after* he died. Standing before the judgment seat of Christ, the man told the Lord that he felt remorse for sins he hadn't repented of during his earthly life and "asked for the mercy of His Cross."[3]

One of our deacons spoke up, disagreeing with the concept of repentance after death. I agreed with him. Tom merely smiled, shrugged his shoulders, and revealed his lack of concern by dispersing several copies of the book, urging all the leadership to take its message to heart and adjust our doctrine accordingly. He later announced a series of home group meetings to implement its teachings. At least one teenage attendee subsequently sought aid from another of our leaders, understandably distressed with Joyner's depictions of demons riding on the backs of Christians while they urinated, vomited, and excreted upon them.[4] According to Joyner, these warriors of darkness had convinced those believers that the slime covering them was the anointing, and influenced the sincere but deluded brethren to wage conflict against other Christians.

This book was taught as the Word of the Lord for his people, with no serious crosschecking with Scripture. Once I became familiar with the basic tenets of Latter Rain doctrine, condemned by the Assemblies of God in 1949,[5] I realized this little volume bore all the movement's earmarks.

Text or Pretext, Depending on Context

The preceding paragraphs underscore a major problem that exists even today within my former congregation. Despite all the books, teaching tapes, experiences, and discipleship materials, New Covenant Fellowship is biblically illiterate, as is so much of the charismatic realm with which I have long been acquainted. This will no doubt spark a barrage of protests, as the Bible is cited profusely in defense of everything from the current contrived spiritual warfare to false prophecy. But a real test for spiritual maturity is not how many individual Scriptures a person may know, but how they understand those same Scriptures in context. Removed from the rest of a passage, one text can become the gateway into a limitless variety of counterfeit doctrines. When I finally put aside all other books and began reading the Bible by itself, proof texts I had used to justify several aberrant positions jumped out at me in sharp correction, one after another.

Take for example that famous line from Isaiah, "Here am I; send me." That statement standing alone, our congregation (and countless others like us) took it as an evangelistic calling from the Most High. When He asked for volunteers to go out into the world, Isaiah cried out in response. We should do likewise, the story goes, and so take the Gospel message to every corner of the globe.

The problem is—this is not a call to evangelize. Read in its entirety, this passage says something startlingly different:

> Also I heard the voice of the Lord, saying, Whom shall I send, and who will go for us? Then said I, Here am I; send me. And he said, Go, and tell this people, Hear ye indeed, but understand

not; and see ye indeed, but perceive not. Make the heart of this people fat, and make their ears heavy, and shut their eyes; lest they see with their eyes, and hear with their ears, and understand with their heart, and convert, and be healed. (Isaiah 6:8-10)

This is not a message of evangelization, but judgment! The people of the Lord, who had received the two tablets of the Law written by the very finger of God, had become so dull of hearing, they could no longer understand simple spiritual principles. Isaiah was not sent to tell the nations surrounding Israel the good news; he was sent to tell his *own* people that they had become blind to the Word of God! Jesus echoes this same observation in Matthew 13:14, when He said "And in them is fulfilled the prophecy of Esaias."

Wrested from the safety of its context, Isaiah 6:8 has become a modern call to preach the Gospel. Granted, the Gospel needs to be preached, as commissioned by our Lord; but when Scriptures such as this one are continually altered from their intended meaning, our understanding becomes distorted so that we hear what we want to hear, not what the Bible actually says. How many would cite this passage with such vigor if they knew the reply is to a call to preach judgment?

We also often cited the famous, "Ask of me" verse from Psalm 2:8, in reference to ourselves. While the passage deals with God the Father speaking to the Son, we removed Jesus from the picture and filled the spot with the church instead. It was another point in favor of the great last day's overcoming army—us, while the truth of the matter is that God's millennial reign on Earth will only be established after Jesus returns.

There are lots more examples of doctrines being built on misinterpreted Scripture, but you get the picture. It is an old rhyme but true that a text taken out of context becomes a pretext … to do just about anything that fits in with your plans.

Round and Round We Go

Great fear and stubbornness surround the pastorate of the average charismatic River congregation. Questioning doctrine, no matter how bizarre, is tantamount to questioning God and eliciting His judgment for our presumption. Or perhaps there arises an attitude from something more basic than that. I believe most pastors, Tom included, have a real desire to participate in everything that will "advance the kingdom of God on earth." The drive to become involved in new things keeps the excitement level high. Tom Smalley in particular had come from a church background he described as dead legalism. Held back from the freedom of the Spirit, he and his congregation were stunted in growth and understanding, and man-made dogmatism had replaced the living Word of God. Therefore, since receiving the "baptism of the Holy Spirit," as Tom put it, and vacating his former fundamentalist pastorate, he opened himself to any experience that had the scent of a fresh wind blowing.

While his zeal is admirable, it became as suffocating as the theological quicksand from which he had escaped. He ran his ship with a maximum of control, and would patiently tolerate little interruptions of his pursuits. When I questioned a favored doctrine or the integrity of one of the many prophets we followed, Tom's wall would come up in a heartbeat. Instead of closely scrutinizing my concerns, he usually just recommended a book to read, of course one written by the author supporting Tom's own position. Too often my misgivings were chalked up to spiritual immaturity, a lack of discernment of the ways God currently chooses to move. The sad part is that I believed it.

Needless to say, the leader's attitude squelched reasonable dialogue. Again, I didn't want to read a book—I wanted to search the Scriptures! Why had that desire been perceived as threatening?

The answer seems to be a foregone conclusion. Our prophets are bringing us messages from God for our time, and we disobey God if we reject them. This is circular reasoning, as that is exactly what is in question, *are these prophets speaking for God?*

The point should be clear. Without firm adherence to objective truth—the Bible—we have no scale on which to weigh doctrine at all. One man's guess becomes another's rigid belief. We are tossed back and forth like a rudderless ship on a stormy ocean, with a broken coastline looming dead ahead. Many Christians have become bored with the simple Gospel truths of salvation, resurrection, and eternal life through Christ. And the rapture is too distant for many to wait for. They have become like the cynics in II Peter 3:3-4:

> Knowing this first, that there shall come in the last days scoffers, walking after their own lusts, And saying, Where is the promise of his coming? for since the fathers fell asleep, all things continue as they were from the beginning of the creation.

Heaven Can't Wait

We are taught by much of the modern church not to look too far ahead; it's *now* that counts. Salvation's a done deal, heaven is assured, and as heirs to the kingdom, its privileges are ours on demand. We have forgotten the words of our Lord, "My kingdom is not of this world" (John 18:36).

The works of Kenneth Hagin, Kenneth Copeland, Benny Hinn and many others claiming the rights of heaven on earth were widely disseminated within New Covenant Fellowship. Books, videos, and cassette tapes routinely made the rounds of both leaders and the average member, sparking predictable awe and a rush to emulate. If they could do it, we could do it. After all, they said so. Our congregation had all their instruction manuals; all we had to do was follow the formula. We looked forward to face-to-face encounters with the living Christ, as they had. And some of our group claimed to have them, at least in visions. Seeing a woman dance on thin air, as Kenneth Hagin insisted in one of his many astounding proclamations, would surely bring in the masses for *conversion*.[6] Living sickness-free every day of our lives (more Word of Faith), would be ample evidence to the world that we were a blessed people. When our earthly vaults overflowed with the world's wealth, we would demonstrate the provision of God. Proof texts made spiritual giants of us all. Laying on of hands, personal prophecy, casting demons out of one another, and "speaking things into existence" made the whirlwind of doctrine all the more exciting.

How Straight the Plumb Line?

Sometime in the early '90s Kris and I were offered an opportunity to travel to a major city for a special time of teaching at a Vineyard church. We gladly accepted, for we were curious about the state's largest metropolitan area and looked forward to some serious additions to our spiritual diet.

Based on Amos 7:7-8, the teaching was called, *The Divine Plumbline*, by Dr. Bruce Thompson.[7] It mostly took place in the local Vineyard meeting area, at circular tables set up with about five chairs at each one. It was an odd arrangement for a church service, conducive to an unthreatening church experience I was told, but I couldn't help feeling like I was in a downtown coffeehouse. And what was supposed to be a biblical teaching took much of its basis from modern psychology, which spoke of "authority figures," "infantile reactions," "social symptoms," and "personality profiles." There was a considerable measure of Scripture throughout the series of videos we had to watch, but the mixture of its application with basic psychological tenets made the teaching thoroughly confusing when looking at it from a strictly biblical standpoint.

The entire purpose of the teaching was to help us differentiate between God and our parents (authority figures). The premise was that we often view God through the lens of the harshest of our parental guardians, warping our view of God. That may sometimes be true. But psychology, birthed in a pagan environment by ungodly men cannot aid in restoration of the human heart. That is the work of the Holy Spirit; and since the dawn of time, He hasn't needed to rely on psychological manipulation or understanding. His power is enough to change anyone willing to submit to God, without regression into the hurts of a painful past.

The biggest problem that emerged for me prior to the ministry time, was that I had no need to forgive my father, whereas others there seemed to need to do just that. In fact, it was the reason we had all gathered together, which I did not know before attending. One pastor there that evening was a man in his late forties, crying and speaking in a child's voice asking "daddy" (his earthly parent) to forgive him for hating and walking in bitterness.

But I had made my peace with my father years earlier, and honestly harbored no ill feelings toward him. I had fully forgiven him, and God had fully forgiven me. Yet while I was never bullied into it, I was strongly encouraged to participate in the forgiveness/repentance process by those in charge. Confused and not wanting to be left out or disappoint God, I confessed something anyway, although not unforgiveness, and was prayed for appropriately.

Ministry time was marked among those present by holy laughter, one of the leaders being stuck to the floor in a heavy sense of what we took to be the anointing. We were awed, believing God had shown up in a powerful way. As I now look through Bruce Thompson's book, I marvel at the causes for apprehensions I didn't heed. But when you paint over that warning light on your dashboard, you convince yourself that all is well—till the oil runs out of your engine and you're left stranded alone on a deserted theological highway.

A House Divided

Just prior to his leaving New Covenant in 1999, Tom Smalley purchased many copies of a book for distribution to the congregation, especially leadership. Utilizing the famous prayer of our Lord out of John 17, the book's premise was that the unity of believers will bring about or hasten Christ's return to the earth. This is a very common notion these days, that Christians are actually preventing the Second Coming by our refusal to lower doctrinal walls. The dismantling of doctrinal caution has been a strong move within our community for a number of years, with the once-monthly exchange of pulpits by pastors in the local Ministerial Alliance. We at New Covenant were consistently encouraged to attend these united services, where those from every congregation in town would gather to worship together.

While on the surface, ecumenical unity seems desirable, in reality walls help to keep good things in and bad things out. I am not necessarily a proponent of denominationalism, as I believe all true Christians worship the same God, regardless of the title we place on our group. But tearing down of denominational boundaries straight across the board has been a most successful tactic utilized these days to introduce heretical doctrines into church fellowship. This kind of contrived unity short-circuits honest discussion and refutation. If I can't speak about what I believe for fear of offending you and neither can you, and neither of us can break company with the other no matter how false our personal doctrines, then this unity is not what Jesus prayed for. Any true fellowship is based not only on love but on truth. While some doctrines are not directly related to our salvation, others are. For example, a true representation of Christ is essential, and anyone who presents *another Jesus* (as I believe leadership in the River movement does) should be avoided (Romans 16:17-18).

It is laughable to think that we as the church are actually capable of holding back Christ's return. Such harmful doctrine is the height of pride. The time is already fixed (Acts 1:7), and no amount of disunity or anything else is going to alter that date one iota. This notion is merely one more rung on the super-spirituality ladder that the uninformed Christian is prodded to climb by church leadership involved in false doctrine. It is another tenet of Latter Rain doctrine. I can say flat-out that refusal to participate in united gatherings will garner the wary believer his share of frowns and disapproving head shakes. It was quite common for Kris and me to suffer a bit of browbeating from the pulpit (although we were never named outright) when we didn't make it to a prescribed service.

When you read John 17 in context, you see that unity is based on truth—in verses 16 and 17, Jesus prays: "They are not of the world, even as I am not of the world. Sanctify them through thy truth: thy word is truth." Unity has to be based on the truth found in the Word.

As for the true unity Christ spoke of, it has already been accomplished. We are already in Him (Ephesians 2:5-6, I John 5:20), and we can't get anymore unified than that.

Spiritual Gifts for the Unbeliever?

Our studies of the gifts of the Spirit, as related in Romans 12 and I Corinthians 12 and 14, led to a desire for positive identification of them among us. As we all moved in one or more of the "giftings," we felt we needed to know which were most prominent in our lives in order to fully accomplish our personal and corporate ministries. Our search was quickly answered by a several weeks' course in "motivational gifts." This presentation led to all kinds of strange ideas and self-proclaimed elitism. Several of the teaching's premises were faulty from the outset. It claimed our gifts were placed within us, even in the womb, an insupportable doctrine on two fronts. For one thing, although Psalm 139:13-16 is used to back up this statement, nothing at all in this scripture even addresses particular gifts. And second, spiritual gifts are not even given to a believer until he *becomes* a believer! Ephesians 4:8 tells us that when Christ ascended, He gave gifts to men. In Ephesians, the people addressed and referred to are Christians, those who have already by faith received Christ as Savior and Lord. Only those included in the New Covenant qualify for gifts. I Corinthians 2:14 states that the unregenerate man *cannot* receive that which is of the Spirit, for those things are foolishness to him.

To teach that unbelievers can carry around the gifts or anointing of God goes against every New Testament passage describing God's outpouring of grace. If unbelievers can operate in any kind of "motivational gift," then we must also give credence to psychics who claim a prophetic call from God. One Vineyard prophet even taught that God had anointed the Beatles with the gift of music that would be used to usher in a worldwide revival.[8] God supposedly lifted that anointing in 1970, only after witnessing years of the Beatles' debauchery and public hatred for Christianity. There is nowhere in the Bible that supports this idea that everyone, saved and condemned alike, has spiritual gifts or a certain anointing residing in them from birth.

Another faulty premise teaches that our individual gifts color our perceptions and actions. Again, this has no place in Scripture. Prophets may prophesy, but that powerful gift doesn't give them leeway to abuse or act in a way contrary to biblical character. Every scriptural command still applies, however a man may see himself, and a true prophet speaks the unsullied words of God.

Scripturally speaking, no spiritual gift should color our perceptions. Our understanding of and interaction with the world should be based upon our relationship to Christ—nothing more or less. For example, we were taught prophets tend to be loners because of their gift. Such assumptions can become an excuse to live in ways contrary to Christian conduct. The excuse, "Well, I don't like to do this or that because my gift is…" has compartmentalized our church interaction.

Also, this idea that we own the gifts as part of our makeup has led to tremendous abuse within the church. Sometimes people who have no concept of the prophetic are suddenly declared, or based on test results declare themselves, to be prophets. Then a hierarchical structure is erected according to how spectacular or "needed" a particular gift is. In our case, as we considered ourselves a prophetic church, a prophet was certainly the recipient of great honor and attention. Test results firmly declared my wife to be a perceiver (changed in the presentation from the biblical term prophet). As our leadership encouraged her to take up that mantle, she often spoke "prophetic words" to people with whom she prayed. She would also see pictures she believed were given her by the Holy Spirit, and prayed for others accordingly.

Once we began our research into this area, she was forced to conclude she assumed a role contrary to God's call of ministry for her. Although sometimes she was perceptive, other pictures she saw while under the anointing were often contradicted by future events, and thus rendered unbiblical.

Condemnation for the Elect

Undue stress placed on the believer to attend multiple mandatory meetings is at best an identifying mark of an authoritarian church structure. At worst, this characteristic is cult-like and mirrors the hierarchical manipulation in groups like Mormons, the Jehovah's Witnesses, and the Moonies. While not technically mandatory, New Covenant's heavy schedule of classes and home groups was so promoted by Tom Smalley that lack of interest on anyone's part, especially leadership, was frowned upon and often criticized. Kris and I were on the receiving end of Tom's criticism, often in the presence of witnesses, for our failure to attend any number of meetings or classes. The stern admonition from the pulpit, "You need to be there!" was a frequent reproach directed toward the negligent member. Although probably done with our best interests at heart, the actual result was condemnation and control over those not adequately responding.

Al Dager makes an interesting and valid observation of this kind of pastoral attitude in his book, *Vengeance Is Ours:*

> Pastors often don't understand why their congregants aren't as committed as *they* are to the church. They wonder why others can't make all of the meetings or get involved in all the things pastors like to see their leaders involved in. What those who make such demands seem not to realize is that it's easy to make the church one's life when the church is the provider of one's livelihood. It's another thing to have to work in the world every day, meet the needs of personal and family obligations, and still give a substantial amount of one's income and time to the church.[9]

Since many of our meetings and programs were based on the doctrines of false prophets and false teachers anyway, I can only say that my disregard in this area worked to my and my wife's benefit.

Jesus' Vision?

Some of the strangest discussions we had in the eldership forum or leadership meetings involved the way Jesus Christ saw Himself. It all started in a concept of the word *vision*, which many in charismatic circles had been kicking around for years. Having a vision for yourself or congregation meant being able to picture the accomplished task set before you by God. It amounted to a combination of desire, goals, and the particular outcome for which a believer is striving. In other words, if someone could visualize something strongly enough, it must be real.

As erroneous as this doctrine was, we further compounded it by suggesting that Christ practiced this kind of visualization Himself. I remember an afternoon eldership meeting in February 1996 where an analysis of the life of Christ "revealed" to us that Christ had a vision for His earthly life. This vision was "seeing Himself as the Son of

God come to destroy the works of the devil."

Do you see what has happened here? Jesus has suddenly become one of us! We need to take a step back and think for a moment. While we, as mere humans, visualize our goals and how to reach them, to arbitrarily place Christ in the same frail position is a farce. While He was indeed fully human, He was also fully Deity. Jesus didn't need to "see Himself as the Son of God." He was, is, and ever will be God Himself.

While it is true that there was a plan for redemption "from the foundation of the world" (Revelation 13:8), Jesus, God in the flesh, did not pursue His earthly ministry within the same framework as we do. His purpose was written in heaven before the earth was breathed out of nothing. Everything He ever did was pre-ordained and unstoppable. Our ministry, on the other hand, is subject to all manner of personal hang-ups, fleshly desires, altered directions, and situations completely beyond our control.

Just Another Brother

This idea of majoring on the humanity of Christ was later developed more fully with the introduction of two messages preached by Tom Smalley in June and July of 1997. Having been given some material from the ministry of once-popular speaker Randy Shankle, Tom proceeded to preach it to the congregation.[10]

Due to Shankle's peculiar view of the Greek meanings of the words sons and children, we were told by Tom that being born again and adopted into the family of God was merely the beginning. Supposedly, we could not walk in the fullness of our biblical inheritance (authority, power, godly character) until we matured into our "sonship" status. A good father, he said, does not give millions of dollars to undisciplined children, but only to those with the maturity to use it properly. While this thought has merit, it encounters some contradiction in the Scriptures. The prodigal son (Luke 15) was not exactly of the responsible sort, nor was he even the eldest (who was evidently the most mature and steadfast in his father's service). Yet the father, a type of our heavenly Father, gave the younger his inheritance, and probably with the full knowledge that he would squander it. In the end, the son returned and repented, had the best robe put on him, his feet shod, and the ring of authority placed on his finger.

According to Shankle's/Tom's teaching, even our Lord was not exempt from having to enter into His inheritance: "Jesus did not come into the fullness of His Sonship until He was anointed by the Holy Spirit." Tom stressed other things that brought into comparison Christ's human nature with our own. That Jesus' earthly life was only lived in the human sphere Tom noted with "He was choosing to live as a human being, not as a half-human, half-God," and it was by drawing on the power of the Holy Spirit within Him that He resisted sin.

This last sentiment had been echoed in at least one other recorded New Covenant sermon, when Tom Smalley stated without hesitation that "Jesus could have chosen to sin." Again, consider the implications of that statement. Could the very Son of God, being God Himself clothed in flesh, have been able to commit sin? This is a horrifying suggestion. The Bible says that God cannot change (Malachi 3:6, Hebrews 1:12, Hebrews 13:8, James 1:17). It should be very evident that Jesus could not have sinned, for He could not deny Himself and His very nature (II Timothy 2:13).

During my twelve years at New Covenant Fellowship, we were taught that Jesus walked the earth only as an anointed man, motivated and empowered only by the Holy Spirit. The Holy Spirit performed all the miracles through Him, kept Him from sin when He was confronted by temptation, and raised Him from the dead. These ideas, although certainly not new, were popularized through television personalities like Benny Hinn and Word of Faith superstars Kenneth Copeland and Kenneth Hagin—who, it will be remembered, downplay Christ's death on the Cross and shed blood for the atonement of sin. Hinn has said in his best-selling *Good Morning, Holy Spirit* that Jesus was moved only by the Holy Spirit and that, had not the Holy Spirit been with Christ, he could have sinned.[11] Hinn also stated, and I have the video of him doing so, that since Jesus was an anointed man, and Christians now have the same anointing, we are now little gods on the earth.[12]

Reality check, please! Hinn speaks of Christ as though, during His time of walking the earth, He was separate from the Holy Spirit, or could act independently of Him. This is ludicrous. Jesus' very nature was one with the Holy Spirit, and He could have done nothing apart from Him—certainly not sin! Self-proclaimed Holy Ghost Bartender Rodney Howard-Browne (laughing revival instigator and major catalyst for the Toronto Blessing) has taught that Jesus was just a prophet walking under the Abrahamic covenant.[13] It is impossible, in view of these teachers' proclamations, to estimate the number of individuals who have been affected. Their ministries reach world-wide and influence believers greatly.

It was reiterated constantly during my time at New Covenant Fellowship that we have the same anointing as Jesus because we are filled with the Holy Spirit just as He was. Of course, our leadership said, Jesus never sinned, but it was because of His constant reliance on the Holy Spirit. When Tom Smalley said that "Jesus chose to walk this earth as a man, not as a half-man, half-God," he was overlooking the fact that yes, Jesus was fully man, but not *just* a man. He was fully God even as He walked the earth. He was clothed with flesh, taking on Himself an additional nature, without any diminishing of the nature of His deity. That is the crux of the matter. He was the Word made flesh (John 1:14) in whom dwells all the fullness of the Godhead in bodily form (Colossians 2:9). His deity was merely clothed or covered over with flesh, not laid aside, as some teach. This was demonstrated on the Mount of Transfiguration (Matthew 17) when His deity shone forth as He prayed and spoke with Moses and Elijah.

Some teach that although Christ did not lay aside His deity, he did lay aside his privileges as deity (the working of miracles, etc.). But although He said that He performed miracles through the Holy Spirit, He also said He performed miracles through His own deity: "Destroy this temple, and in three days *I* will raise it up" (John 2:19, emphasis mine). Scripture teaches that God raised Jesus from the dead (Acts 2:24, Acts 2:32, Acts 3:15, Romans 10:9, and lots of others), and that the Holy Spirit raised Jesus from the dead (Romans 8:11). Jesus also stated in John 5:19, 21:

Then answered Jesus and said unto them, Verily, verily, I say unto you, The Son can do nothing of himself, but what he seeth the Father do: for what things soever he doeth, these also doeth the Son likewise.... For as the Father raiseth up the dead, and quickeneth them; even so the Son quickeneth whom he will.

So, the Father works miracles, and Jesus works miracles. Plus, He cast out demons by the Spirit of God (Matthew 12:28), yet the demons knew Him to be Christ and that He had the power to destroy them and cast them into the abyss (Luke 4:34-35, Luke 8:31). The important thing to remember is that the Father, Son, and Holy Spirit all work together, in agreement, in unison—all the time. They do not work independently of one another. That would explain why some miracles were credited to the working of God, some to the Son, and some to the Holy Spirit. Also, we know that we are purchased by the blood of Christ, but in Acts 20:28 we are told we were purchased by the blood of God. Father, Son, and Holy Spirit—inseparable, in complete union, one.

The Devil Made Us Do It

The main question that causes confusion is: If Jesus was fully God with all the attributes of undiminished Deity, then how could He be tempted? What was the purpose of the temptation in the wilderness?

Two things need to be borne out—one is that it was the Holy Spirit Who led Jesus into the wilderness confrontation with Satan, and that the temptations took place, not to see if Jesus would sin, but to prove that He couldn't. Although as a man Christ could be tempted, as God it was impossible for Him to yield to it. Remember, He never surrendered who He was as God, He simply added flesh to who He already was (John 1:14). If it was possible for Jesus to sin, then He did walk only as a man filled by the Holy Spirit, which is what much of the charismatic world believes. But if it was possible for Him to sin, this would mean the changeless God (Malachi 3:6, James 1:17, Hebrews 13:8) could change. James says that

God cannot be tempted by evil (James 1:13). God cannot lie (Hebrews 6:18). James 1:14 is a very telling verse —"But every man is tempted, when he is drawn away of his own lust, and enticed." Did Jesus have any lust or inordinate desire where He could be drawn away from God and enticed? Absolutely not. Christ—God and man—was perfect and sinless. And though he could feel the disgust at the temptation, there was no enticement there. It simply couldn't touch Him.

One more thing mitigates against Jesus' walking only as an anointed man while on the earth—this is the presupposition that if we also rely on the Holy Spirit as He did, we can walk without sin. This is a basic Latter Rain heresy, and it goes way back to the gnosticism of the first century. I have personally spoken to a gentleman who belongs to a wilderness group formed by self-proclaimed apostle and prophet Sam Fife in the 1970s.[14] He told me that sinless perfection is not only a mere possibility but a biblical promise, and it will eventually culminate in physical immortality—prior to the general resurrection at the second coming of Christ. It didn't seem to matter too much to him that none from his group (or any other Christian group for that matter) has ever attained to sinless perfection or immortality. He was convinced it was God's will for sinless perfection and present immortality to occur in Christians who truly follow Christ and know the secrets of discipleship. What he forgot is that John's epistle states that if we say we have no sin, we deceive ourselves, and the truth is not in us (I John 1:8). Everyone sins, and in many ways (James 3:2), but not Jesus. He is the unique Son of God, and God the Son. He could not sin.

This in no way threatens our love for Christ or our belief in His sharing our sufferings and having experienced the same kinds of temptations we have. On the contrary, it should make us feel even more secure in Him, knowing that He was and is a Savior that nothing can alter.

While Tom Smalley did qualify his beliefs by affirming Christ's uniqueness, the whole issue was muddled with repeated comparisons between the believer and Jesus.

As much as Christians are often guilty of doing so, we cannot equate ourselves or our ministry with that of the Son of God. Although as believers we are certainly commissioned with His authority, it belongs to Him, not us, and it is by His power, not our own, that we minister. Although He took human form, He remains the eternal God. The chasm between our created makeup and His Deity is infinite. To try to close the gap by any means is the same kind of folly first committed in the Garden of Eden.

The God of All Grace

This bare sketch of New Covenant Fellowship pursuits is merely the tip of the theological iceberg. Materials from Kenneth Copeland, Kenneth Hagin, Roberts Liardon, Jesse Duplantis, Benny Hinn, John Wimber, Rodney Howard-Browne ... the list just goes on and on. Feasting on the fantastic, our appetites were never quite sated. We were always left craving just one more spiritual high brought about by the *newest* teachings, tales of the miraculous, and face-to-face encounters with God, angels, and demons. No claim was too wild for us to believe. From the prophetic to the power signs, this religious wild goose chase made certain we always had our running shoes on, ever ready to sprint in whichever direction the spiritual wind happened to be blowing at the moment. As a result we had become "children, tossed to and fro, and carried about with every wind of doctrine" (Ephesians 4:14). What would have happened if we considered for a brief moment that maybe, just maybe, these teachers on whom we showered adoration (and finances) weren't telling us the truth?

It amazes me even today that God did not abandon us through it all. Like Israel of old, perhaps there were still enough morsels of shining truth in that carnal mess of pottage that kept us from completely apostatizing. At any rate, it was surely unfathomable mercy of God.

> Go and proclaim these words toward the north, and say, Return, thou backsliding Israel, saith the LORD; and I will not cause mine anger to fall upon you: for I am merciful, saith the LORD, and I will not keep anger for ever. Only acknowledge thine iniquity, that thou hast transgressed against the LORD thy God, and hast scattered thy ways to

the strangers under every green tree, and ye have not obeyed
my voice, saith the LORD. (Jeremiah 3:12-13)

Acknowledge. That is the key. Admit the wrong, confess the sin,
repent of the iniquity and disobedience, the chasing after false gods
that cannot satisfy. Until we admit there is a problem, that we have
left the narrow way to get caught in the traffic jam of perdition, then
we have no hope of ever finding our way out. Fear of discovery is the
tether that holds many a pastor and church member in bondage to false
doctrine. The need to publicly confess perhaps years of promoting
false teaching from the pulpit and in home groups can paralyze the
most ardent of believers.

Although the truth does sometimes wound, it also heals. And
once proclaimed in the sight of all men, the truth is the fortress to
withstand all the enemy can throw at it. Loss of position, friends, or
congregants means nothing when it comes to being found on the side
of the Master. It is only in the truth of the Scriptures that we can be
assured of our eternal place beside Him.

Then said Jesus to those Jews which believed on him, If ye
continue in my word, then are ye my disciples indeed; And
ye shall know the truth, and the truth shall make you free.
(John 8:31-32)

Slavery to false doctrine or freedom in
Jesus Christ—the way, the truth, and the
life (John 14:6). We must decide—which
is it going to be?

CHAPTER 7

THE (VERY) LAST LAUGH

> "Close your eyes, raise your hands;
> when you do the power of God will fall on you!"

It was an amazing spectacle. The church carpet was strewn with sprawled bodies, some on top of one another. Various individuals wept as in mourning; some shook uncontrollably, limbs twitching in powerful spasms. Others stumbled "under the influence," unable to put one foot in front of the other in a straight line. Some were caught up in the rapture of full-color visions. The majority reeled from unstoppable laughter, faces red and hands over cramping stomach muscles, many sliding to the floor in a disheveled heap in front of or underneath the pews. The din was phenomenal. Like a kind of hysterical battleground, this bedlam of unrestrained emotion had claimed its fallen warriors.

And all we did was follow directions from the man in the pulpit.

Welcome to the Party

Although we at New Covenant Fellowship had never previously witnessed anything like "holy laughter," the doctrinal groundwork had been already laid. We *knew* that the cutting-edge church was always the first to experience the mighty, mysterious work of God, and we received this latest move with open arms. The power was almost inconceivable—never before had so many been laid out by the "touch of God," been caught up in ecstasy to the heavenly realms, and known such joy and release in His wonderful presence. As we constantly lived on the brink of every new manifestation of power, we were ripe for a "fresh anointing," a wind that would sweep into the congregation and, through us, out into our town.

In the early 1990s, Pastor Tom Smalley invited an evangelistic team to New Covenant. Having traveled and ministered with God's Bartender himself, some in the group had received the impartation of spiritual drunkenness and holy laughter. Consisting of two key speakers the first time, the team came to our little rented church building near the outskirts of town. It was too small for us, even in the early days. Meant perhaps for a congregation of fifty, the building was packed out by our group of about seventy-five.

The acknowledged head of the team was Jim O'Brien, a young, good-natured fellow whom the Lord had rescued some time earlier from a life of involvement with the occult. His sidekick was a broad-shouldered linebacker type, Walt Lightoller. Amiable enough when out from behind the pulpit, he preached with an intensity that, matched with his incredible physical presence, could be a bit intimidating.

Jim spoke for a good portion of the church service. Calling one of our members up to the front, he demonstrated the "nature" of the Lord "as He lives within the believer." Standing side-by-side with the other man, Jim said, "Lift your right arm."

As he did, Jim also lifted his. Told to move his leg, turn around, walk across the floor, Jim matched every move made by our church member. The whole idea was that, whatever we do, the Lord within us also does. He never leaves us for a moment, occupying by His Spirit our vessel of flesh. I don't recall exactly where he was going with all this, except to let us know that God is in us, and to prepare us for what was to follow in the service.

There's only one point I'd like to make at this juncture. It is obvious that, although the Holy Spirit does indeed indwell us wherever we go, He certainly doesn't participate in any works contrary to His nature, whether we do so or not. If we choose to indulge our flesh, we do it on our own. To say that He lifts His arm when we do, etc., is to perhaps suggest something a bit more far-reaching than the Scriptures would allow.

While the content of the sermon eludes me, I do remember Jim telling the story of his having breakfast with Rodney Howard-Browne after a ministry session in one of the bigger cities. God's Bartender reached across the table, touched Jim and said, "Have a double dose! [of the power]."

Jim politely smiled, felt nothing, and continued chewing. About a half-hour later, Jim felt somehow different. Attempting to stand in order to pay the check, he found his legs would not cooperate. His speech slurred, the words came thick and slow. Staggering so badly he could not walk, he had to be carried by one man under each armpit up to his motel room where he could wait out the effects of the anointing.

Jim had been hit with spiritual drunkenness.

This particular demonstration of power took place in a public forum, outside the comparatively accepting confines of a church service. To the world witnessing this, Jim looked like a drunk who had to be bodily carried from a nearby barroom. In all my years of enjoying "drunkenness in the spirit," I never once considered that someone in that reprehensible condition could minister for the Lord Jesus Christ. As a wise former pastor of mine once told me, "Just try witnessing to an alcoholic with a beer in your hand."

The implications are clear. A lover of alcohol will laugh in your face and despise the Gospel if he sees you proclaiming Christ while in a condition similar to his own.

When the message was over (in anticipation of the manifestations—we couldn't wait for the preaching to end), Jim began to call people forward for prayer. Flanked by Walt, Jim laid hands on everyone who wanted to receive a touch from God.

The congregation was told to lift hands, close eyes, and expect the fire of God to fall.

And what we believed was the power did come nearly every time, with instantaneous effect. Immediately the noise became absolutely unbelievable, with uproarious, uncontrollable laughter the most prominent response. Everyone seemed to be having a great time, lying in the pews and rolling on the floor in happy convulsions under the "power of God." Demons were addressed and supposedly fled, and those who had been harassed by them set free. Some healings were apparently manifested. God's visitation had come, and we went out to tell the town.

Reeling Them In

Folks from other congregations began attending the twice-daily meetings. If they were predisposed to believe as we did, many experienced the same manifestations. One nightly service involved an entire line of people being slain in the spirit at once, falling into the aisle one atop another. In one such pileup, I dropped early, but although the power had knocked me down, it seemed somewhat deficient when it came to making me comfortable with the heel of a fellow inebriate's shoe digging into my body. Mercifully, someone came by to rearrange limbs so that those on the carpet might have a few square inches of uncompromised floor space.

Not everyone agreed that such a fiasco was God, but New Covenant members were undeterred. We weren't about to reject any means by which God chose to move, no matter who was offended or how strange the manifestation.

A very good friend from a local evangelical church came one evening to check things out. Her pastor husband, a wonderful Christian man who had befriended Kris and me years earlier, could not attend the service. This gentle lady's obvious lack of enthusiasm for the proceedings did not go unnoticed. When asked by Walt to step into the aisle to receive the blessing, she politely refused, the only one I ever recall doing so. Walt coaxed, but without success. She felt no need or desire to experience an encounter like those she was witnessing.

I am ashamed now to admit feeling sorry for her, that she had shut herself off from the blessing by approaching the experience with unnecessary caution. For me, as for probably most of us in the building, the issue was one of power. Since something was obviously happening, and in a church service no less, then it must be of God. Why fight it? In retrospect, I remember some of the conversations I had with people I tried to persuade to come to the meetings. I mostly spoke of power, not the Gospel that saves men from eternal death. I guess I felt that the average guy on the street wouldn't listen to solid spiritual truth without seeing a demonstration of signs and wonders. Funny, we had forgotten the words of our Lord: "An evil and adulterous generation seeketh after a sign" (Matthew 12:39).

From our first exposure to the manifestation, through our years of attendance, we at New Covenant were hit with about three different episodes of the laughing revival. Since we had no building of our own, the meetings took place wherever our group happened to be gathering at the time. The services were to become a proud part of our Pentecostal tradition within the framework of our new doctrinal understanding.

More Than Meets the Eye

Anyone involved in marketing will tell you that packaging is half the sell. If the wrapper is brightly colored and attractive to the human eye, it will create a desire to purchase. Even if the ingredients match exactly those of a generic brand, the consumer will automatically gravitate toward the more exotic display, believing it to be of superior quality. It is only when the box is opened and the packaging discarded that the contents are found to be the same mundane quality as the cheaper brand.

Translating this into the spiritual arena, a glitzy appearance often *sells* more than the content itself. When superstar televangelist Benny Hinn wows a congregation with an anointing distributed by his breathing dramatically on people or using his arm like a cutlass to slash the air, the packaging looks impressive. The higher the body count, the greater the public draw. But the old adage is true that the proof of the pudding is in the eating. Without the atmospheric lighting, ethereal music, anecdotes, and accounts of the miraculous-fueling expectations, I just wonder how many slain would litter the floor of his church services and crusades.

Even during the most explosive segments of our laughing revival experience, I got the same inkling some things were not quite right in *River* city.

First off, there was the use of the microphone in the meetings. Although the building was small enough for the ministers to be heard clearly from the front, they set up a sound system anyway, complete with speakers that could blast out both music and voice far beyond that required for normal hearing. During the after-the-message melee, I saw and heard one rather innovative use for the sound system. Standing in front of one of the pews while many people were in the throes of the anointing, Kris and I prayed to be touched. With our eyes closed, we heard a sudden, loud rush of wind enter the building and beat against our eardrums. The onslaught was too powerful to resist. At the same time, we both collapsed into a sitting position, landing so hard on the pew that our combined weight nearly tipped it back onto the people behind us. Although the anointing felt wonderful, and frightening in a "holy" way, the base of my spine hurt from hitting the pew. I wondered why it should hurt at all if I was under this anointing, but I kept my eyes closed and did my best to revel in the feeling of glory.

That sharp pain was my first clue.

The next clue came when, upon opening my eyes the second time I heard the wind, I saw that it was not the wind of the Lord's presence, but Jim O'Reilly blowing hard into the microphone. I suppose it was to duplicate the sound of the "violent, rushing wind" heard in the upper room on the day of Pentecost. This practice vaguely disturbed me, but I discounted it as good theatrics to help usher people into the experience.

The third clue sent up red flags when Jim came to personally pray for Kris and me. While we had been enjoying watching nearly everyone laughing themselves silly, all we did was smile. We honestly felt no inclination to break out into laughter, and in fact I had questioned my own maturity when I did not respond to the anointing as I believed I should. I often secretly wondered what was lacking in me that God would pass me by.

When he saw no open manifestation upon us, Jim reached around and placed a hand on either of our heads, calling on God to fill us and bring the laughter and joy into our beings. His hand was heavy, pressing down uncomfortably. He prayed and coaxed us, and after some time we finally began laughing a little, but that was not enough. With a big grin on his face, he coaxed some more. Finally, laughing as much as I could possibly force, I said, "I'm doing the best I can!"

He nodded and walked off, grinning. But I felt cheap. I had faked a laugh, not under the anointing, but manipulation. This persistent coaxing is a hallmark trait of this entire movement. Shouts of "More! More!," "Here it comes!," "Fire!," and a variety of other catch phrases were repeated endlessly over those coming up front for prayer, halting only when the person receiving prayer succumbed or absolutely would not manifest. I saw many of these prayers or commands to receive the anointing fall flat. Some people, although hungry for God, did not manifest at all when prayed for, regardless of the heavy coaching involved. It was embarrassing for the individual who wanted desperately to please, embarrassing for the minister who wanted the display of power, and embarrassing for New Covenant membership because we believed so firmly in the whole thing. We attributed this lack of response to any number of things—other than the possibility that this movement was false.

A Ministry of Violence?

In some various meetings, other things were not adding up. A teenage member of our congregation caught the laughter, and, falling down drunk, was held up in front of the church by Walt and another aide as a symbol of God's power. This young man laughed so hard and so long that a profusion of small capillaries in his face broke, giving him the appearance the next day of someone who had been involved in a fist fight. His stomach ached badly from the convulsions of the night before. Thinking of it now frightens me, although at the time I discounted any physical danger to him in favor of the power of the anointing.

Admittedly, he could well have been faking it for the benefit of friends who had come to the meeting. But he affirmed continuously that he could not bring himself to stop laughing, and it does not seem likely that he would deliberately cause his own injury.

Deliverance, a la Laughing Revival

When Walt Lightoller separated from Jim O'Brien to form his own ministry, he came again to our church, which by that time was housed in a rental facility that accommodated various community workshops and church services. Within the large adjoining auditorium, normally reserved for local stage performances, one of Walt's meetings had much of the same flavor of the spiritual chaos to which we'd grown accustomed. There was the average hysterical laughing, slain in the spirit, and one young lady stuck to the floor, but one incident in particular stands out in my mind. Attired completely in black, a young woman known in our town to be a practicing occultist came to the meeting at the urging of her sister, who was a member of our congregation. Arriving after the message had been preached and the manifestations had begun, she found herself singled out by Walt, who recognized the demonic in her. As he approached her at the front of the auditorium, she backed away in wide-eyed terror, emitting one short, piercing scream. Flat against the wall, she could retreat no farther, and Walt commanded the spirit to depart. Others gathered to pray for her as well. After some intensive warfare praying, she was pronounced clean.

"Are you happy?" Walt asked.

The young woman nodded with a smile.

"Then why don't you praise God in a dance?" he suggested.

She flitted around the front of the auditorium for a moment with hands in the air, while the crowd that had gathered to witness the exorcism stood behind her. It was precisely for that reason they could not see her eyes. As I sat in one of the front rows, she passed within fifteen feet of me and the vacant look in her eyes did not speak to me of joyful deliverance. My impression was that she was unchanged, merely biding her time until she could safely make it to the nearest exit. To the best of my remembrance, we never saw her at church again, and afterward she remained deeply involved in occult practice.

You Did *What* in Church?

Certainly the most disturbing incident occurred during one of the first meetings Walt conducted apart from his former partner.

Walt had brought along with him a young man scarcely out of his teens to lead worship. Housed at Pastor Tom's residence, this young man woke up Saturday morning and found himself mute. Tom recounted the story the next day with obvious enjoyment. Toward the end of the evening, the silent youth had his speech miraculously restored, and so could lead Sunday worship. No explanation that I can recall was given for the apparent muteness, only that it was a demonstration of the power of God.

After the Sunday service, with many in manifestation on the church floor, the worship leader himself hit the carpet, the lower half of his body protruding into the front of the sanctuary, and his head slightly inside the open doorway leading to the pastor's office. His breathing came in long, drawn-out sighs between clenched teeth. His face turned a frightening beet red. What I must describe now will be offensive, and for that I ask pardon. With his breathing coming in greater and more pronounced gasps and his face livid, he writhed on the floor and ran his hands up and down the sides of his body, eventually pushing himself with contorted body movements halfway into Tom's office area.

Most of the congregation was gathered at the back of our church building. I sat saucer-eyed, alone in the front pew, staring with mouth hanging open and my mind in a confused whirl. All the previous training I had received to expect anything from God could not begin to prepare me for what I was now witnessing. Stunned, I could not take my eyes off him. The gesticulations, the heavy breathing, the grotesque facial contortions bore the marks of what looked for all the world like sexual passion. If I had seen this anywhere else but in the sanctuary of a church, I would have believed it to be open perversion.

Noticing my discomfort, Walt Lightoller and Tom Smalley sidled up to me. "It's okay," Walt soothed. "He's just under the anointing."

Afraid to disagree for fear of speaking against the work of God, I hid this particular event in my heart. It would not be until years later that I found the courage to bring it out into broad daylight for honest evaluation.

Law of Diminishing Returns

Many of the manifestations that accompany a movement like this begin with a roar and end up with a whimper. At the beginning, it resounds magnificently within church sanctuaries, but after a while it becomes commonplace. It just doesn't have the *zing* it once did.

The same is true of laughing revival power. Just a year or so after Jim O'Brien and Walt Lightoller split up their team to pursue separate ministries, Jim returned to New Covenant for a series of meetings. Though the promise of getting a fresh touch drew many to hear his sermons, people just weren't stumbling over themselves like they once did. In fact, there was little real manifestation of any kind. Despite his continuous refrain of "Drunk! Drunk in the Holy Ghost!," the spiritual drunkenness characteristic of his prior meetings didn't materialize. He spent a great deal of time on individuals who came forward for the anointing. With hand laid on him or her, and praying out loud for the filling, Jim coaxed, coached, and, possibly without being aware of it, manipulated with phrases like, "There it is [meaning the anointing of power]! Take it! Take it!"

Yet, despite all this prompting, very few actually hit the floor slain in the spirit or "drunk." It seemed that all the original fanfare accompanying the manifestation simply didn't wow us too much anymore. Let's face it—when you've run the gamut of power, the same old thing just doesn't quite intrigue as it once did. Like everything else, it will grow uninteresting when compared to the newest manifestations.   The same is true now for the Toronto Blessing. With the grand sweep of manifestations now ebbing quietly away, church leadership once associated with the movement is beginning to come forth with poor explanations. In the wake of mass confusion over the withdrawal of the power, excuses like, "God's season of powerful manifestations is ending. Now He is drawing His people into the wilderness" have been making the rounds. It's ironic that, when the manifestations are going full-tilt, they are an all-important sign of the working of God among His people. When they fade, it seems they never were that important anyway. The standard of faith and practice is constantly shifting, for convenience's sake.

But I guess that's what it means to go with the flow of this new river.

What Saith the Scriptures?

It is rather pointless to attempt construction of a biblical framework for what our congregation experienced. In the seven or so years since Kris and I had our first taste of this form of "renewal," the scriptural justification for the party atmosphere is just as nil now as then. All manner of convoluted interpretations of Jesus' words or the writings of the prophets have been used to prop up a display of unabashed carnality in the only place a person should be able to escape it—the church of Jesus Christ.

Having been an ardent supporter of the holy laughter movement perhaps gives me a one-up on those who have only viewed it from the outside. I can state with finality that based on my personal observations of the movement's inner functions, its source could not be God. Much of what took place and still does is largely the work of man. In my years at New Covenant, I have been part and parcel of emotional manipulation, heightened expectation, atmospheric maneuvering, and precious little solid biblical teaching. The fact that a genuine power at times does seem present does nothing to ease my concerns; in fact it does just the exact opposite. Whatever spirit it is that makes folks drunk and lose all inhibition, fall atop one another in a tangled mass of arms, legs, and raised skirts, laugh without restraint in the middle of a solemn church service or at communion (the remembrance of our Lord's sacrifice), and disparage the word of God that was delivered once for all to the saints for their protection—is *not* the Holy Spirit.

If these things happened in a bar, we as Christians would be rightly appalled. But when they occur, and continue to occur with practiced regularity in the very sanctuary of our churches, then we are expected to look on with indifference and believe that somehow—in some unfathomable way that was never revealed by our Lord, the apostles, or the prophets of old—that God is at work. The righteous horror at such fleshly exhibition has faded in the growing shadow of popular Christian myth, fulfilling the Scripture "[A]nd the people sat down to eat and to drink, and rose up to play" (Exodus 32:6).

As Moses stood with the law of God in his hands, he looked with rage on the exposed flesh of his people—staggering drunk, chasing one another with unbridled lust, dancing with mindless abandon before a god of their own making, and claiming it was he who had given them commandment to party.

Why is the truth so hidden from our eyes? If it is disgusting to see a grown man slobber on his shirt due to an extended stopover at the bar, then why is it appropriate to see his Christian counterpart likewise out of control? We reprimand the brother or sister who drains the bottle, who neglects wife and family in order to binge, but we commend that same believer who imbibes at "Joel's Bar"[1] and must literally crawl on hands and knees to find his way home. We mourn the brother who is too drunk on natural ferment to start his vehicle, but when a church has "designated drivers" for congregants who are too out of it to put the key in the ignition, we smile warmly and sigh, "Praise God for His refreshing!"

The comparisons are striking. The only difference is in where a person gets loaded.

Of the 40 biblical references to laughter, 22 of them refer to scornful laughter and seven refer to Abraham and Sarah's disbelief about her late in life pregnancy. Of the remaining references, there are virtually none that speak of laughter in a positive sense, with perhaps an exception in Psalms 126:2 (when the captivity of Zion was over and David said "then was our mouth filled with laughter and our tongue with singing"). According to former New Age follower, Warren Smith (who wrote a powerful critique on the holy laughter movement) "the only three references to authentic laughter in the New Testament—warn AGAINST laughter."[2] Smith states:

> These three references actually seemed to underline Solomon's contention in Ecclesiastes that "sorrow is better than laughter" and that now is a time to weep and not to laugh. In Luke 6:21 JESUS says, "blessed are ye that weep now: for ye shall laugh." In Luke 6:25 JESUS says, "woe unto you that laugh now! for ye shall mourn and weep." James 4:9 tells us not to laugh but to "be afflicted, and mourn, and

weep: let your laughter be turned to mourning, and your joy to heaviness."[3]

Smith evaluated the laughing revival from the standpoint of the New Age:

> A number of Christians have experienced the equivalent of "holy" laughter when they were in the New Age. Indian Guru Bhagwan Shree Rajneesh was affectionately known by his followers as the "divine drunkard" because he was reputed to have drunk so deeply from the well of the "Divine."
>
> As a former follower of Rajneesh I met hundreds of Sannyasins who had flown to India "to drink" from "Bhagwan's wine." When followers were physically touched by Rajneesh, or even if they were merely in his presence, they would often experience feelings of great exhilaration and joy. Disciples of Swami Baba Muktananda would often manifest uncontrollable laughter after receiving Shaktipat (physical contact) from the guru.[4]

This is no laughing matter. Even should most of this movement prove to be more a work of the flesh than demonic activity, we should never forget that our Lord hates carnality. Although it is an extremely unpopular message these days, fleshly abandon in the name of the Most High God cannot be sanctified or made contextually holy. "Because the carnal mind is enmity against God" (Romans 8:7).[5]

We need to take a long, sober look and avail ourselves of God's wisdom given to a former hater of the church, Saul of Tarsus. Considering himself the least of the apostles (Now that would be a novel idea among today's self-appointed apostolic company!), Paul reminded the Corinthian congregation that they needed heartfelt repentance. All their presumed spiritual power and pride had corrupted the very idea of what they were supposed to be—ambassadors for Christ—and had likely rendered them a laughing stock among their pagan countrymen—as it has ours. God's truth for them is still truth today and should be heeded:

Having therefore these promises, dearly beloved, let us cleanse ourselves from all filthiness of the flesh and spirit, perfecting holiness in the fear of God. (II Corinthians 7:1)

CHAPTER 8

"I Just Had a Vision!"

"Jeanette has seen two angels in the building, one standing at the front door and one at the back. They have come to praise the Lord with us!"

There is perhaps nothing so powerful as a vision. When the heavens open and our eyes look upon fantastic things once hidden, it can alter the course of our lives:

> In the year that king Uzziah died I saw also the LORD sitting upon a throne, high and lifted up, and his train filled the temple. Above it stood the seraphims: each one had six wings; with twain he covered his face, and with twain he covered his feet, and with twain he did fly. And one cried unto another, and said, Holy, holy, holy, is the LORD of hosts: the whole earth is full of his glory. And the posts of the door moved at the voice of him that cried, and the house was filled with smoke. Then said I, Woe is me! for I am undone; because I am a man of unclean lips, and I dwell in the midst of a people of unclean lips: for mine eyes have seen the King, the LORD of hosts. (Isaiah 6:1-5)

A glimpse into heaven itself to behold the God of all flesh made Isaiah panic with self-loathing. His innermost heart was revealed in the light of the Lord's glory, and there was no place to hide.

Who wouldn't want to have a vision of this magnitude? And why shouldn't we? On the day of Pentecost, the Christians present experienced the outpouring of the Holy Spirit: "[A]nd your young men shall see visions, and your old men shall dream dreams" (Acts 2:17).

Never in the history of our planet have so many who call themselves Christian claimed visions from God. Encounters with Christ, angels, demons, even saints long departed have begun to appear in book form, crowding the charismatic section of our local Christian bookstores. The popularity of visions never seems to wane, and the more a person has and the greater the scope, the quicker he is skyrocketed to Christian stardom. People with virtually no genuine theological training are suddenly propelled into the teaching arena, regaling vast audiences with tremendous accounts of their own spiritual derring-do. And while the stories continue to scale the heights of plausibility, an amazed public looks on, vicariously a part of the panoramic excitement and often with hands folded atop a closed Bible in their laps.

Sadly and without exaggeration, the above account is an apt description of the spiritual maelstrom that always characterized New Covenant. Sunday services were routinely stopped to give opportunity to report a vision that occurred during worship. Many in the congregation would listen with rapt attention as one person after another would share what had transpired "in the spirit." Sometimes demons would make an appearance; sometimes it was the Lord Jesus Himself.

Angels were a particular favorite. I can't tell you how many times angels have made an impromptu appearance at our services. The opening quote in this chapter offers a typical sampling. Jeannette McElroy seemed graced with multiple visitations. On this particular Sunday afternoon, Jeannette had gone up to the front of the sanctuary, in the middle of a worship song, to speak privately with worship leader Beth Clayton, Pastor Phil's wife. Beth held her hand over the microphone, listened momentarily to Jeannette, and then nodded. At the end of the song, Beth in triumph noted the presence of the two angelic beings seen by Jeannette. They were there to worship with us, she exclaimed, and she led the congregation into a brief period of shouting praise to God for sending His angelic emissaries.

No one halted the festivities to suggest examining the claim in the light of God's Word. It was merely taken at face value and used to bolster our self-image as the church on the cutting-edge of God's worldwide movement. By then several months into my own charismatic research, I exchanged a brief, frustrated glance with Kris.

When I later brought up the angel incident in an eldership meeting, Beth staunchly denied she'd promoted the vision. She maintained she had merely acknowledged Jeannette's word and left it to the congregation to decide its veracity. But my wife and I were both there. The way it is described above is exactly the way it happened. Interestingly, none of the rest of the leadership in the room nixed Beth's version, despite the fact that some were present during the "angelic visitation."

Tunnel Vision

The cries of "I saw!" reverberated throughout New Covenant Fellowship my whole tenure there. Sometimes the visions were two-dimensional, sometimes 3-D, and sometimes the person was actually caught up into them, in the same way the apostle John was translated into the heavenly realms in the book of Revelation. They moved as participants in the vision itself, walking, feeling, etc. As Pastor Tom consistently reminded the congregation of its prophetic calling, dreams and visions grew to paramount importance. They were used to chart our congregation's very course, and any resistance or verbal doubt was severely frowned upon or openly dismissed.

Never having been much involved with either prophecy or visions, I had no foundation of experience from which to judge. I left the decision to the rest of the leadership, to accept or reject whatever came forth with the label of vision. Finally, during my last year as elder I did my own Bible study on the subject, and what I discovered left me angry, frightened, and delighted. Angry, because I felt we had been duped personally and congregationally. Frightened, because so many visions were coming forth on a regular basis with no real safeguard as to their origins. Delighted, because I was no longer held captive by supposed visions from God, which I had long suspected were other than from Him.

Many people cannot appreciate the gravity with which visions are accepted in many charismatic/Pentecostal circles, and consequently cannot understand the bondage that results. If someone has a vision of "the Lord Jesus" and is given a message to convey to you, for you to treat it lightly is to despise the very words of God. You are bound to carry out the instructions of this visionary or face the consequences. The ensuing fear can be devastating, especially if the message contradicts your own conscience or understanding of the Scriptures.

The new believer is especially vulnerable because he is led to believe that all these visions are from God. Furthermore, any hindrance to, or lack of visions on his own part is due, he is told, to lack of maturity and failure to fully trust the leadership.

Accepting everything that comes down the pike as from God is like driving a car while wearing blinders. You can't see the big picture. Your actual focus becomes so constrained that you miss necessary landmarks to indicate proper direction—not to mention the fact that sooner or later you'll get sideswiped by a vehicle you never saw coming.

On the Wings of Angels

At my best count, there are less than thirty visions or dreams recorded in the entire New Testament, and of these only about fifteen took place in the book of Acts. And this in a period, from the birth of Christ to the last chapter of Acts, encompassing about sixty years.

I have come to the conclusion that visions are not the norm for a believer, but a rare occurrence. Of those saints in the Bible described as having bona fide visions from God, a mere handful had more than one recorded vision in their entire lifetime. Furthermore, none of these occurrences were initiated by the individual, but were the result of a divine act of God. In explaining mystical experiences, which is the category visions fall into, I like this explanation by research analyst Ray Yungen:

While certain instances in the Bible describe mystical experiences, I see no evidence anywhere of God sanctioning man-initiated mysticism. Legitimate mystical experiences were always initiated by God to certain individuals for certain revelations and were never based on a method for the altering of consciousness. In Acts 11:5, Peter fell into a trance while in prayer. But it was God, not Peter, who initiated the trance and facilitated it.[1]

Compared with the frequency of modern visions by many charismatic churchgoers, these past biblical heroes seem almost deficient in their relationship to the Lord.

Concerning the visitation of angelic beings themselves, the scriptural record directly conflicts with such experiences. In our own meetings, those with frequent visions of angels had often depicted them as merely standing around, enjoying or participating in a worship service with us. Contrast this with the biblical model of angelic visitation. In both Old and New Testaments, angels are beings sent by God to give verbal messages (often concerning the future), to administer divine judgment, to strengthen and comfort, and to give specific direction, warnings, and deliverance from dangers. Their appearing was an amazing event; fear was the natural human reaction to their presence, or at the very least an awed respect. Visions of angels in the church of today, however, nearly always produce glee or a giddy joyfulness, little awe, no fear, and often the "angels" are just standing enjoying themselves and have no message from God. In heaven this may sometimes happen (we simply don't know), but the scriptural precedent demonstrates their earthly visitation always heralded a direct message from the Lord and their very presence caused an immediate shock to the person witnessing it. In those times when angels hid their identity (Genesis 19) they were viewed as mere men, and when they made their identity known, the reaction was fear, shock, and awe.

Likewise, visions of any kind, in both Old and New Testament, appear to be very rare occurrences. Acts 2:17 has been used to support the argument of increased occurrence of visions in the end-times, but the context of Scripture shows that we have been in the last days for the past two thousand years. If anyone should have had a preponderance of visions, you'd think it would have been the apostles, who knew the Lord Jesus face-to-face and wrote the New Testament under the inspiration of the Holy Spirit.

All in the Mind?

I believe that most of what are reported as visions are not such at all, but could be more appropriately termed mental pictures. The two are certainly not synonymous. Mental pictures occur constantly during our waking hours but don't necessarily have anything to do with the spiritual, whereas visions always have their origin in the supernatural realm. As we speak in conversation, we see mental images, memories, etc., to correspond with the dialogue; reading gives us the same experience. Even television viewing offers the same scenario, as the images dancing across the screen click on our own past experiences or connections with our present situations. This can transpose into our times of prayer, giving us mental pictures that may or may not be of God.

This conclusion really upset my wife Kris (the first dozen times I mentioned it!) because she had often relied on mental pictures as a guide when praying for others. Encouraged by the leadership as prophetic, Kris watched the pictures that arose in her mind for clues to the spiritual condition of the person she was praying for, and the subsequent remedy.

After personal Bible study and serious prayer, she came to question this method and eventually discard it as a valid practice in ministry. The practice itself can be dangerous, actually maneuvering an innocent Christian in the wrong direction. In many cults, and, unfortunately in much of the Pentecostal arm of the church, it has already done just that.

That is not to say that all images we see are wrong. Some may be quite correct at times. But "[w]e have also a more sure word of prophecy; whereunto ye do well that ye take heed, as unto a light that shineth in a dark place" (II Peter 1:19). The Word of God is the mirror in which to examine all our practices, thoughts, deeds, and desires. If God had left anything out of His written record, the void would allow all manner of personal interpretations or inventions to prosper. The resultant chaos would cripple any objective discernment.

Snapshots of Eternity?

Although perhaps not genuinely classed as visions, photos of *Jesus*, angels, even people hovered over by *spirits of death* have been showing up in the last few decades. One of the most highly respected prophets of the 20th Century, William Branham, has been photographed with a spiritual fire flowing over his altar, a nebulous presence standing beside him on the platform, and in his congregation, a church member hooded over with a death mask. I examined all these photographs on a website devoted to the man, and frankly, it was chilling.[2] The pictures reminded me of my days in the New Age movement, ghost-hunting and spirit-seeking, and the photos I had seen of those supposedly long-dead. I got much the same feeling from looking at the Branham pictures.

We need to do some critical thinking at this point. How can a material lens and film capture the likeness of a spiritual being? Has the entire world been lacking this proof of the spiritual world prior to the invention of the camera? One photo kept in New Covenant's office was reportedly of Jesus Himself. Taken out of an airplane window, it showed a nebulous figure of Christ standing on storm clouds. It was rather impressive—to a people of unquestioning faith in nearly all visions—and remained among our office effects for some time.

Did we believe it to be genuine? Why else would we have kept it and showed it to others?

On Closer Examination

In all my years at New Covenant, I recall only once when a vision by a leader in the worldwide prophetic movement was questioned. In one of the many prophetic conferences followed closely by Pastor Tom, some of his favorite speakers made some rather startling proclamations. The audience was told to "Forget balance!" in this final hour, and to receive what the prophets had to tell. And tell they did—of visions of angels sweeping into the convention center complemented by portions of prophecies that were contrary to Scripture. Thankfully, these sent up a few red flags to some of us at the leadership meeting. Tom wanted to disseminate the transcript of this prophetic conference among our membership, and with an open show of regret he acquiesced to the reservations of the few of us who spoke out.

As far as I know, Tom did not dispose of the transcript. He simply told us that he would not give it to the congregation at that particular time. It is also very telling that, despite uttering serious deviations from the Scriptures, the prophets at that particular conference were still highly regarded by New Covenant leadership. But then, that was normal practice since our congregation submitted to the spiritual authority of the "last days apostles and prophets."

This irrational clinging to the coat tails of big-name prophetic ministers short circuits the ability of many congregations to reason things out. God is not opposed to common sense; the book of Proverbs bears that out. Just because Oral Roberts told the world that he witnessed a 900-foot-tall Jesus lift the City of Faith doesn't mean we have to take his word for it.[3] Rick Joyner's claim to put a vision on hold while answering the phone should trigger spiritual alarm bells.[4] Visions of angels entering a conference room and touching people to imbue them with uncontrollable holy laughter should be closely scrutinized, no matter how famous the visionary.

II Corinthians 11:14, Colossians 2:18, and Galatians 1:8, might very well be applicable here. Over the objections of the current prophetic element in our midst, we must recognize the necessity of standing firm against anything that does not match up with Scripture. The body of Christ has been reeling from the last two or three decades of purported visions from self-proclaimed seers—men and women who have largely succeeded in altering the longstanding orthodox stance of the church. The frightening, unquestioning overall acceptance of their words has led many to depart down a multi-lane highway away from recognizable Christianity.

Quality Testing

According to the Bible, there are three sources of visions—God, the devil, and the flesh. Of these, only one can be trusted as to motive and authenticity. As for the other spiritual experiences originating with the kingdom of darkness or human sensuality, they must be discarded, and immediately. They are not impotent fantasies, but are corrupt from the word go and will quickly lead astray anyone whose attraction they capture:

> Thus saith the Lord GOD; Woe unto the foolish prophets, that follow their own spirit, and have seen nothing! O Israel, thy prophets are like the foxes in the deserts. Ye have not gone up into the gaps, neither made up the hedge for the house of Israel to stand in the battle in the day of the LORD. They have seen vanity and lying divination, saying, The LORD saith: and the LORD hath not sent them: and they have made others to hope that they would confirm the word. Have ye not seen a vain vision, and have ye not spoken a lying divination, whereas ye say, The LORD saith it; albeit I have not spoken? Therefore thus saith the Lord GOD; Because ye have spoken vanity, and seen lies, therefore, behold, I am against you, saith the Lord GOD. (Ezekiel 13:3-8)

I cannot stress this enough—contrary to popular fallacy, there is no such thing as a *harmless* false vision. Its fraudulent nature alone is enough to condemn it in the eyes of God; those who give ear to it will eventually have their faith in Christ contaminated, perhaps shipwrecked. Attendees of the Peoples Temple were regaled with stories of angelic visitations and "revelation knowledge." The reverend Jim Jones capitalized on his self-proclaimed intimacy with heaven to lead a group of followers into mass suicide in the Guyana bush.[5] Don't think that the average believer in Christ is immune to this kind of deception. In the wake of gold teeth and gold dust *miracles* showing up in various River congregations worldwide, stories of angel feather sightings have set a portion of the charismatic church wild with jubilee. One West Coast church said that "tiny white feathers and gold flakes" appeared during the service.[6] Such occurrences were the next logical step in an already deception-heavy system of super-spirituality, rationalization, and the frenzied pursuit of illusion.

While there could be genuine godly visions that do take place today, they are very rare and not apt to guide people into the fantastic or to gather a following. Contrast this with the nearly cult status accorded some presumed seers, who not only relate a plethora of dreams and visions that contradict biblical foundations but who make a rather decent living doing it through books, conferences, special engagements, etc. The overused mantra of "God is doing a new thing and therefore the Scriptures don't specifically address it" should be relegated to the ash heap. Any true heavenly vision may only confirm what is already in the Scriptures:

> To the law and to the testimony: if they speak not according to this word, it is because there is no light in them. (Isaiah 8:20)

Do not go past that which is written. Through Scripture, the Holy Spirit repeatedly makes the same statement in manifold ways:

> These were more noble than those in Thessalonica, in that they received the word with all readiness of mind, and searched the scriptures daily, whether those things were so. (Acts 17:11)

> But evil men and seducers shall wax worse and worse, deceiving, and being deceived. But continue thou in the things which thou hast learned and hast been assured of, knowing of whom thou hast learned them; And that from a child thou hast known the holy scriptures, which are able to make thee wise unto salvation through faith which is in Christ Jesus. All scripture is given by inspiration of God, and is profitable for doctrine, for reproof, for correction, for instruction in righteousness: That the man of God may be perfect, thoroughly furnished unto all good works. (II Timothy 3:13-17)

A master of camouflage, "Satan himself is transformed into an angel of light" (II Corinthians 11:14). We are admonished to put to trial those things we see or hear claiming to be from the heavenly realms:

> Beloved, believe not every spirit, but try the spirits whether they are of God: because many false prophets are gone out into the world. Hereby know ye the Spirit of God: Every spirit that confesseth that Jesus Christ is come in the flesh is of God: And every spirit that confesseth not that Jesus Christ is come in the flesh is not of God: and this is that spirit of antichrist, whereof ye have heard that it should come; and even now already is it in the world. (I John 4:1-3)

To confess means to agree with. Any spirit, vision, dream, prophet, experience, whatever, that does not agree with the revelation of Jesus Christ as set down in the Scriptures is not of God. Water may look pure, but unless we know the source from which it is drawn we may drink to our own ill health. A close examination with a magnifying glass may betray bits and pieces of debris, or worse yet, organisms roaming its depths that, taken internally, would cause debilitating disease.

Am I suggesting we carry around a magnifier to inspect anything coming our way? Perhaps that is just what is needed. For too long, we've covered our eyes with blinders instead and accepted a testimony to our detriment, simply because the person giving it named Christ and seemed sincere. Paul said even deceivers within the church would attempt to pass themselves off as the real article (II Corinthians 11: 3-4, 13). We can judge without being judgmental. Peripheral issues we can overlook, knowing full well the sole reservoir of truth does not rest with us.

But in the presentation of Christ, there can be no leeway. A false image of the Savior—His character, words, or deeds—will lead us away from the truth, and consequently, away from God. And eventually, that is what every fraudulent vision will do—take away from the person of Christ and demand our attention and adherence to its personalized message. I have seen it happen, as one vision after another proclaimed in my former congregation boosted our elitism and remolded Jesus just a bit more into the user-friendly image we preferred. With virtually no accountability, fear of redefining Christ's biblically revealed character faded bit by bit into obscurity.

Chapter and Verse, Please

Promoted by Tom Smalley, a binder containing the prophecies, dreams, and visions of New Covenant members was put together. Kept for a time at his house, it was open to viewing by any interested party within our group, and open, as well, to the insertion of new material. It was passed on to another church member for safe keeping just before Tom and his wife left for the east coast. The idea behind the volume was to keep track of the way God was speaking to our congregation, and to adjust our attitudes and church direction accordingly. In other words, these recorded spiritual incidents were prayed over, meditated upon, and generally held in high regard, with a view to determining the health of our congregation. If God was indeed speaking through His people, then we needed to heed every word.

The implication here is that God did not give us enough direction in His Word alone to live by.

The Bible offers no precedent for gathering a collection of spiritual experiences and allowing them to determine personal or corporate direction for a body of believers. The only volume we have need of has already been given to us, and it has ably resisted the systematic onslaught from the kingdom of darkness for millennia. To place as much credence on current visions or assumed revelations as we do on the Bible is to add to the canon of Scripture, which we are sternly warned against in Revelation 22:18. While those in the River loudly deny doing so, that is just what has happened. Let's face it—a person either believes a vision to be of the Lord, or he doesn't. If he does, he's bound himself to act on what he accepts as the truth of God—even if that *truth* cannot be precisely located in Scripture. As a product of such an environment, I can state for the record that I saw such contradiction acted out all the time. I was guilty of it myself.

Two years before I left New Covenant, one of our most prominent elders, standing with Pastor Tom, told me unblinkingly, "Some
experiences are so powerful, that you just have to go with them. You
have to put the Scriptures aside until you can understand the experience in the light of the Word." At that time, I was stunned beyond
speaking and recently have begun to wonder how you can simultaneously disregard the Scriptures and yet hope they authenticate an
experience you've already made up your mind to follow.

This current state of things within the church is just the out-
growth of an inner movement attempting to differentiate between
truth and revelation. It is being stated by popular charismatic authors
that truth is where God has been, but revelation is where He is at
the moment. This dichotomy is a contrived one. The Word of God
is truth *and* revelation both, and the timeless truth of God's Word
applies to all saints throughout all ages. Again, the implication of
this kind of compartmentalized thinking is that the Scriptures fall
embarrassingly short when it comes to equipping the saints for life
in today's world.

What should shame us as believers is the wholesale disregard for
the only visible, objective, sure, written Word of God. In our mad
dash to embrace the new thing, we have run right past the only place
of refuge, God's Promise, that can keep us from hurtling down the
face of an impossibly steep cliff. I can testify to the broken lives and
empty spirituality that remains when the initial high wears off. We
had congregation members regularly spending their cash to jet to
this or that prophetic conference. They just had to keep up with the
latest move of God, and bring it back with them to New Covenant.
Running after other gods, ancient Israel attained to this spiritual
bankruptcy on a regular basis. But we can take heart, for their failures
can be our lessons:

> For whatsoever things were written aforetime were written
> for our learning, that we through patience and comfort of
> the scriptures might have hope. (Romans 15:4)

For those former seers willing to swallow a large helping of humble pie, there is most certainly hope. For those willing to repent, the grace of our Lord will lead past every soulish and narcissistic revelation, helping us to walk in humility and the simple freedom of Christ Jesus.

For the rest, the road can only lead further into deception and confusion, compounding itself with every new revelation that adds to, subtracts from, or contradicts Scripture.

> I have heard what the prophets said, that prophesy lies in my name, saying, I have dreamed, I have dreamed. How long shall this be in the heart of the prophets that prophesy lies? yea, they are prophets of the deceit of their own heart; Which think to cause my people to forget my name. Jeremiah 23: 25-27

Chapter 9

Make a Joyful Noise

"These people would stand on their heads if I wanted them to."

I stood near the pulpit during a Sunday morning service, looking out over the congregation with something perhaps akin to awe when this thought first crossed my mind. The looks on their faces, the exuberance, the abandon in worship was something that struck me with startling force. They followed my every move, heeded my instructions, shouted hallelujahs with me and proclaimed any faith confessions that I deemed momentarily appropriate. For me, about a year into my position as worship leader, it was a disturbing instant of realized power.

If the components of a church service followed one another according to numerical superiority, worship would top the list. Even in the most conservative churches, a time of hymn singing is held each week.

And why not? We were made to worship God, to proclaim His goodness, mercy, and justice, and acknowledge even through music the greatness of His salvation through Christ. To the honest, genuine Christian, worship is not only a privilege, but as critical to spiritual health as breathing is to the physical body.

But when man blends his own desires and imaginings with the work of God, corruption with a capital "C" is inevitable.

Before pastor Tom Smalley approached me, I was quite content to simply fill a seat and sing to the Lord from my own heart. I've always loved a good song, and with a practiced voice I could hit a decent range of notes and hold them on a tremble, drawing my share of positive comments. Embarrassed when I turned heads in any kind of admiration, I was quite taken back when Tom asked if I'd like to lead worship for a while. The busyness of the pastoral office was eating away at his time, and being on the worship team added to the burden. At first I smiled sheepishly and dismissed the idea, but when approached a second time and coaxed with a suggestion of God's possible calling on my life, I hesitated but then decided to give it a try.

Though halting at first, I soon grew into the role and was leading worship with confidence by about the third month. By then Tom had stepped down from the worship leader position and was enjoying the song part of the service with his family, encouraging me by looks from his seat and generous amounts of verbal praise afterward. Although plagued by self-doubt and at times agonizing over being in such a position of prominence, I nevertheless grew secretly jealous of my "gift."

It's In the Bible, Isn't It?

Music ministry has now grown to monumental proportions in the church. Not only are there local worship leaders, but there are books, conferences, seminars, and videos to teach the correct application of technique, direction, and atmosphere. Leading worship has come to be one of the key factors in establishing appropriate congregational mood, with the stated intent that the Holy Spirit may not be hindered in His ministry. Some worship leaders have attained charismatic stardom by voice and vivacity, capturing the hearts of assembled believers and leading them into dizzying realms of "intimacy with God" through music. Some have become part of traveling ministries, taking their talent to welcoming congregations worldwide, while others have become the selling feature of a host of audio and video recordings, depicting what is considered true worship in the Spirit. I have heard that some commercial music promoters claim special anointing status, saying that impartations, such as that experienced at the Brownsville Revival, can be realized just by listening to music recorded at that Pensacola church. The *glory cloud* has supposedly come into the midst of some River congregations, and at least one major prophetic voice claims to have seen congregants' hair blowing in "the wind of the Spirit."[1]

One has to wonder where it will all end.

To the best of my knowledge, no scriptural precedent exists for the office or "gifting" of worship leader. It was not a recognized position in the New Testament Church, is not listed in the spiritual gifts categories of Romans 12:4-8, I Corinthians 12 or 14, or Ephesians 4:7-12, and, if the blunt truth be known, is not even a requirement for a functioning body of believers. Congregations around the globe survive quite nicely without the addition of a chief musician or song coordinator.

While not necessarily a bad idea, it lacks biblical validity for the body of Christ and can actually hinder true expression of personal worship. Having been on both sides of the microphone, I can testify that members of the congregation, especially those who have a strong desire for intimacy with God, will follow the leading of whoever stands in front during the song portion of the service. They will do their best to mimic his movements and follow his suggestions, which often have strong hints of coming from God Himself. I would often hush the worship team into a quiet musical interlude while I quoted Scripture, encouraged the congregation, or sometimes called people forward for prayer. Often I laid hands on those who approached at my invitation, and as I prayed, it was not unusual for some to fall out or be slain in the spirit. Sometimes a touch wasn't even necessary; merely passing by them provoked the same response.

Where's the Focus?

The point is, I was closely watched because it was widely believed that up front, where the power was supposed to be concentrated, I clearly heard and followed the direction of the Lord and ushered the congregation into His presence. However, for the most part, I cannot even honestly say that I did. I certainly tried, and believed I heard Him, but to punctuate the moving of the Holy Spirit with dubious manifestations seems at best contradictory (James 3:11-12). I wonder now how much was Spirit-led and how much was carnal choreography. I recall every Sunday studying the faces in the congregation for signs of boredom, distraction, interest, or rapture, and sometimes adjusting technique accordingly.

There had to be wholesale involvement by the people, or I felt personally deficient or even angry that they weren't responding to what I perceived as God's presence. And of course, without actually soliciting comment, I kept my ears open for any remark praising the content of that day's worship service. It goes without saying that any worship time enlivened by multiple manifestations was a feather in my cap. After all, if our group worship and the "manifest presence" of God were virtually united, and if worship was good that day, then certainly I was instrumental in bringing the people into that place of experience.

Is this shameful? Yes, and it should be, and I would hazard a guess that many of my former peers indulged the same feelings. I need to say here that not everything was done with wrong motives, nor do I believe most other worship leaders desire to manipulate. We longed to see God move, to have a touch from His hand, and if we could see what we believed to be a supernatural response with our own eyes, then it was a token of His personal affection and a confirmation of our ministry. But we would have done well to heed the admonition of II Corinthians 5:7: "For we walk by faith, not by sight."

Like so many other areas in Christendom today, the worship of God has become tainted with the cravings of the flesh.

Could You Repeat That, Please?

Of all the techniques used in many worship services, perhaps none is better known than the repeat chorus. Engaging the method myself during the two years I led worship, I quickly wearied of it after I stepped down, noting that even good songs thus conducted took on a monotonous quality that could not be scripturally accounted for. Beginning a song with a fair amount of enthusiasm, my interest would wane to the point of tedium if the song continued unremittingly, and in exasperation I would simply sit down, unfortunately drawing attention to very nearly the only one in the building apparently not committed enough to stand while praising. And a church elder, at that!

While I honestly loved God and desired to worship Him, I discovered, at least for myself, that heartfelt closeness was being replaced by what I can only term charismatic ritualism. Depending on the song, I could tell at a glance roughly how many times the chorus would have to be sung before it was felt the people had "entered in" and we could move on to the next one. It was said regularly that believers coming into the service were either inner court, outer court, or holy of holies Christians, each one needing a certain period of time to come into the manifest presence of God. The longer a chorus droned on, or the more often it was repeated, the more time was allowed for the slower believer to shed the cares he'd come with and leave the mundane world behind.

I wonder just how much credence this technique deserves. Do we all need an hour of repetition in order to draw near to God? Seems that the times I've been in rebellion have been the times I've heard God the loudest. Falling into sin and becoming discouraged, I have heard the quiet comforting voice of the Good Shepherd leading me back to the straight path, encouraging me to repentance and a restoration of joy. The prophet Jonah was stomping mad during his recorded discourse with the Lord (Jonah 4) yet had no trouble discerning the voice of Almighty God. By our present standards of worship, he wasn't anywhere near ready to come into God's presence!

It occurs to me that Jesus had something to say about this very scenario:

> But when ye pray, use not vain repetitions, as the heathen do: for they think that they shall be heard for their much speaking. (Matthew 6:7)

Something repeated often enough can easily become meaningless. Just ask any parent who's had to correct a child about the same thing for the thousandth time.

Wild and Crazy

These days it is fashionable among many charismatic groups, and certainly those in the River, to direct congregations into an intense emotional state via music. While emotions of themselves are God-given and good if held in proper context, like anything else feelings can be given too much free rein. Misdirected spiritual hunger can produce a desire to throw off all restraint, and music can be the inducement. A quick glance at a rock concert crowd is very revealing. Hands in the air, bodies gyrating, and fans screaming in ecstasy are all the standard. Whipped into a frenzy by loud, pulsating music, they become unhinged, adopting a different model of behavior because of the atmosphere.

As much as we would balk at the suggestion, the same basic mood pervades many congregations during worship time. Both the Brownsville Revival and the Toronto Blessing are noted for the unbiblical manifestations that often follow an extended song session. I can personally attest to the power of music, joined with high intensity preaching, to induce a vibrant expectation among church membership. A portion of a Benny Hinn crusade that took place in 1999 ably portrayed this very thing.[2] It was frightening to watch on video. Hinn paced wild-eyed back and forth on stage under what he claimed was the anointing, roaring "Fire on you!" at participating pastors, the choir, and those who came up for prayer. In a deep, gravelly voice completely unlike his own, he rebuked supposed demons of illness and imparted his fire anointing, strewing bodies all over the stage. At one point, he looked dramatically heavenward, said, "Yes, Lord, I'll do it," stretched forth his hand and proceeded to place a curse on everyone who would speak against his ministry. All the while, as the atmospheric music played quietly in the background, the faces of the huge congregation were rapt, awestruck, the eyes of some brimming over with tears as they witnessed what they truly believed was a holy man "under the anointing" of God.

Take away the music, the lighting, and the grossly exaggerated showmanship, and perhaps someone would have recalled the words of the Master in Luke 6:27-28:

But I say unto you which hear, Love your enemies, do good
to them which hate you, Bless them that curse you, and pray
for them which despitefully use you.

Through stage manipulation, a multitude had been led to believe
that the same Lord who gave this tender injunction would now command Benny Hinn to wreak havoc upon his enemies.

Sour Grapes

During the time of the laughing revival outbreak, New Covenant
Fellowship made "The Glory is Here" our trademark song. Its
powerful nature led to the expectation of more supernatural encounters. It spoke of sensing God's supercharging the atmosphere around
us, and we were encouraged to simply reach out and take whatever
we needed from Him, claiming it as our own. This song initiated
a changeover that was to have long-lasting repercussions, brought
about through the vehicle of Vineyard music. Tom and Sherri Smalley
had for some time been looking at our group becoming part of the
Vineyard movement and having traveled to a Vineyard conference in
the Lower 48, returned sufficiently impressed to proceed. While our
congregation, for one reason or another, subsequently failed to enter
into the movement itself, cassette tapes of Vineyard music began
showing up, along with accompanying song sheets and transparencies
for the overhead projector.

Many of the songs contained a mystical quality, a certain touch of
something that provoked within me a vague apprehension. Immediately,
I didn't care for the majority of the songs, although it was a given that
they were to become a mainstay of the worship portion of our services.
I led worship only a few times Vineyard music was used before stepping down from a position in which I no longer felt comfortable. Phil
Clayton, one day to become pastor, stepped in to fill the void.

I had no solid information about Vineyard at all, only what had
been sketched out briefly by an enthusiastic Tom. I did not know
about the subjective approach to spirituality by Vineyard leader John
Wimber, or the "paradigm shift" he believed was necessary for the

twentieth-century church.[3] Nor did I know that the place the Toronto Blessing broke out was also a branch of the Vineyard.

In the years following the Toronto Blessing (and the deluge of pro-Toronto material via pulpit teachings and monthly congregational subscription to *Charisma* magazine), our worship times were peppered with references to water, often in the form of Vineyard songs. A takeoff from the prophecy of Ezekiel 47, this symbol of the Holy Spirit became our gateway into the supernatural. One song we began singing with monotonous frequency told about a rushing torrent flowing from God to touch those who need reviving. In connection with the River movement, it's easy to see the theological direction the lyrics would tend to lead a congregation. Another song that promoted spiritual drunkenness spoke of God's people asking for a drink of the Spirit, and supposedly being made inebriated with His presence, a practice we've already discussed in detail.

Through the joint medium of music and the worship of God, our already distorted doctrine was conforming to those in the River movement, and it was generally received with abandon. What we were not told (although it would likely have been applauded) is that spiritual drunkenness had so permeated charismatic congregations enamored with the Toronto Blessing that certain worship choruses had been renamed drinking songs, and the churches themselves were being called drinking houses.[4] Debauchery in the temple of the Lord (I Corinthians 6:19) had been given its musical benediction.

The Final *Note*

While we as believers rightly decry the sensuality marking worldly music, we blithely overlook the same trait in our own camps. Music has the power to convey thought, atmosphere, and attitude, and in the church all three had better point us to the Lord or we're wasting our time and dishonoring Him. Leading worship, where the position exists, should be approached with extreme caution and absolute dependence on Christ, knowing the frailty of human nature and our propensity to manipulate. To be sure, people want to be led, and if it is in our power to direct them, the temptation to do so in accordance with carnal perceptions can be a heady draft. Even if the motive on the part of the worship leader is good, constant checking against the plumb line of God's Word is necessary to maintain purity. And humility is not just an incidental; a stark recognition of our own inadequacy and knowing that we fill, in leading worship, a place not even scripturally necessary, will help stave off sensual desires to lead in a direction of our own manufacture.

True worship is not found in fleshly music, bizarre manifestations or mystical, extra-biblical doctrines of self-aggrandizement. It *is* found in the simplicity of Christ, a humble acknowledgment of our rescue from the disgrace and eternal punishment for sin, and the joy of being set free to know, enjoy, and yes, fear the Lord God.

The New Paradigm

"Just take out your unforgiveness, and hand it to me."

Removed from the larger, milling congregation after the service, Jackie Rowan sat on a step at the side of the sanctuary, the look in her eyes alternating between worried resistance and perplexed animosity. Kneeling before her, Beth Clayton prayed quietly and with a "word of knowledge," thought she understood the block that was impeding Jackie's wholehearted repentance. "I know this sounds strange," Beth said, "but I want you to reach into your heart, take hold of the unforgiveness, and place it in my hand."

She smiled, opened her palm and held it in front of Jackie, waiting.

Not knowing exactly what to do, Jackie's eyes flitted from Beth to me, possibly in the hope of finding an ally who would rescue her. Like a coward I said nothing, having already earned a badge of dissidence due to a battery of difficult questions I had aimed at the leadership, and only moments before having preached an unwelcome sermon on the heresy of Word of Faith. I simply prayed that God would somehow intervene in this mess. Jackie had publicly acknowledged that she needed to repent of undisclosed sins, and instead of biblical instruction she found herself the object of psycho-mystical practice.

Finally in desperation and obvious embarrassment, with a quick movement she reached toward her heart to grab the perceived root of sin and placed it uneasily in Beth's hand. "There's a little more in there," Beth said with a smile and to my amazement reached toward Jackie's heart area and supposedly plucked out the remaining bitterness. Closing her fingers over the nebulous handful, she prayed for God to release Jackie from her burden of unforgiveness, and then proceeded to pass her hand over, up, and around Jackie, conforming the movements to the contours of the confused girl's body. The whole fifteen minutes struck me as bizarre in the extreme, and was more reminiscent of New Age energy channeling than godly ministering. Jackie's face registered relief when she was permitted to leave, presumably delivered from whatever had kept her in bondage to sin.

At the time of the above incident, I was already far into my research, recognizing a multitude of practices in our group that had no reference point in Scripture. Although I had not seen this particular hand method used in our group, I had, through video, seen it done by Toronto Blessing leadership. Their technique exactly mirrored Beth's. Ostensibly there was something in the motion itself that helped in the spiritual realm, and it has become quite common among River congregations to incorporate these gesticulations into the course of personal ministry.

More and more it seemed that, even as we gave lip service to the Bible and praised Jesus during our worship time, we were doing what He never did. While we said that Christ alone heals the brokenhearted, we dove headlong into healing aids like psychology, spiritual manipulation, and unbiblical patterns of restoration and deliverance. One minister who made the rounds at New Covenant, a sincere man with a genuine caring heart, stomped his foot repeatedly and maneuvered his neck while praying for others, varying his voice from a whisper to a booming yell when ministering to the same person. Another from a Juneau church writhed strangely while praying, as if someone manipulated her spine, and tossed her head in little jerks. Still another would repeatedly and softly cry out "Oh!" as if twinged with pain under the anointing, involuntarily jerking his head with the utterance. I've seen the same basic manifestation in a more dramatic form, on a video of Carol Arnott of the Toronto Blessing. Her Sword of the Lord Anointing, at a special women's conference, shook her violently while she cried loudly and repeatedly, "Oh!"[1]

It seemed to us at New Covenant Fellowship, and we were told so ad infinitum, that God could do anything—even outside the realm of His written Word. So, no matter how weird the practice, how unfounded the doctrine, if it seemed spectacular and produced even temporary results, it was acceptable.

That was why Beth could feel comfortable pulling unforgiveness out of someone's heart, waving her hands mystically in the air, and believe it was all from Jesus. That's also why River congregants can crunch, dip, roar, bark, *birth* in squatting positions, shake like a rag doll, howl, thrash around on the floor, you name it … and lay claim to the blessing of God on the manifestation. In an eldership meeting just prior to beginning my research into the movement, Beth Clayton said with a chuckle, "If God wants to make somebody cluck like a chicken, who am I to argue with that? God can do anything."

No one disagreed.

John Wimber's Paradigm Shift

The Toronto Airport Christian Fellowship's success on the world stage is best understood within a Vineyard context, as that church was a Vineyard affiliate at the time of the revival's outbreak in January of 1994. It was Vineyard magnate John Wimber who ushered into popularity the term paradigm shift, an idea which brought the charismatic arm of the church to a radically new viewpoint of what biblical practice should entail. A paradigm is an example or pattern, and according to Wimber's purported discovery of the gaping differences between the Middle Eastern and Western mindsets, the Christian West needs to be turned on its theological head. Believers in Middle Eastern countries, Wimber taught, have an openness to the supernatural which allows them to experience personally an interaction between the physical and the spiritual realms. We in the Western world have become so deadened, the theory goes, to spiritual reality, it is difficult and often impossible for miracles, manifestations, and revelations from God to break through. Thus, Wimber says, we need a major alteration in our method of approaching God and allowing Him to approach us. The old study and learn method (commended by the apostle Paul in 1 Timothy 4:13-16, and II Timothy 3:14-17) is no longer adequate. In fact, according to Wimber and a flood of Third Wave teachers, it never has been. Experience is what counts, they say, and all that head knowledge we've been accumulating all these years is a big waste of time. This teaching states that to really know God, His power and miracles, we need to shuck all that dead letter stuff and get into the life.[2]

One of the main problems with Wimber's paradigm is that there is no evidence that any one people group is hindered from believing in Christ and receiving the benefits of His salvation because of a cognitive orientation. Faith comes by *hearing* (Roman 10:17), not feeling. Anyone who receives the invitation of Christ through faith will be saved, as is declared in Revelation 22:17 :

> And the Spirit and the bride say, Come. And let him that heareth say, Come. And let him that is athirst come. And whosoever will, let him take the water of life freely.

Wimber also first introduced into mainstream charismatic congregations the incredibly strange manifestations that are supposedly initiated by the Holy Spirit. Pogoing (jumping up and down in place), rippling on or under the skin, tingling, shaking, convulsions, uncontrollable laughter—many of the same kins of manifestations traditionally attributed to demonic influence—have now attained prominence in River meetings. Former New Age medium Brian Flynn, in his book *Running Against the Wind,* describes what is known as the Kundalini Effect, which takes place during deep eastern-style meditation. It is shocking and frightening to see the similarities between this and Wimber's manifestations:

> Symptoms can include headaches, nausea, tingling sensation, and uncontrollable twitching. The Sanskrit word Kundalini means the curled one, and is also called Kundalini awakening or the awakening of the serpent. Practitioners describe it as a curled channel in the tailbone area. It can rise through the

chakras (psychic centers situated along the spine from the tailbone to the top of the head), creating physical symptoms ranging from sensations of heat and tremors to involuntary laughing or crying, talking in tongues, nausea, diarrhea or constipation, rigidity or limpness, and animal-like movements and sounds.[3]

How is it that River revival movement signs are no different than the demonic symptoms described by Flynn? And yet, it is taught that those who *don't* experience these to some degree are rather deficient in their ability to receive God's "manifest presence." Although this too will be vehemently denied by a verbal majority in the River, that same majority calls the inhibited Christian "hard to receive." I know. As a member of New Covenant leadership I knew it to be standard policy to downplay the spiritual maturity of those who resisted or criticized these manifestations. We figured that if God was moving in our midst only spiritual babes, or those bound by fear or legalism, would be unable or unwilling to enter in and appreciate the wild goings-on in our meetings. And while we would listen to the teaching from the pulpit, it was widely recognized that it was merely a precursor to the real excitement, such being ministry time.

John Wimber's dependence on experiences to define spirituality is summed up in one overused word—fruit. Basically the idea is that if someone was hanging from the ceiling for hours during a spiritual encounter, we are not to judge the experience immediately, but rather look at the person's fruit. If the individual claimed a deeper love for Jesus after the experience, that would be enough to validate its being from God.

Where is the plumb line of God's Word in all this? In a 1983 Vineyard leadership conference, John Goodwin quotes Wimber as saying: "All that is in the Bible is true, but not all truth is in the Bible. We integrate all truth, both biblical and other, into our experience of living."[4]

As a self-described former Vineyard pastor for eight years who often accompanied Wimber on his travels, Goodwin notes that the *fruit* of this spiritual smorgasbord is partially the result of Wimber's borrowing theological thought from such notables as Agnes Sanford and meditation promoter Morton Kelsey. Having twice read one of Sanford's books called *The Healing Light,*[5] I can attest to its gross New Age content. It is replete with such ideas as thought vibrations, visualization, metaphysical healing techniques, and positive confession. Kelsey, in *Healing and Christianity,* equates the ministry of Jesus with shamanism,[6] commends encounters with the dead as natural spirit-earth links,[7] bases much of his book on paganistic Jungian psychology, and calls the atonement a "hypothesis developed" by the early church.[8]

With this anything goes mentality, the playing field is wide open. In one of our Sunday afternoon meetings, the wife of one of our elders shook, cried out, and fell unmoving to the floor. Pastor Tom Smalley strode forward from the pulpit, looked the congregation right in the eye, and said, "If you don't like what just happened here, then you've got a religious spirit, and you need to get rid of it!"

Kris was livid. By this time, she knew a work of the flesh when she saw one.

The bottom line was that a manifestation could not even be questioned without the inquirer's spirituality being put on trial.

Disparaging and adding to the Word of God in River groups is common in the extreme. How many times have we heard that "God is bigger than His Word?" According to Goodwin, Wimber used the term often.[9] Such reasoning sets up a false conflict between the Word of God and the Holy Spirit! How can God act outside the boundaries of His own written proclamation to His own covenant people? One of the main reasons for covenant is to assure that both parties will know what to expect from each other. If God were so completely unpredictable as those in the River assert, then what is the sense of even having the Bible? It becomes merely a convenient guidebook at that point, an elastic text with as yet unwritten pages.

Caught Up ... In Deception

Since the first century church, believers have looked ahead to the gathering of themselves to Christ at the rapture. While there is a difference of opinion on the timing (pre-tribulation, mid-trib, and post-trib), the general consensus has been that there will come a time, already appointed, when Christ will descend, and Christians, both alive and asleep (dead), will be caught up in the air, "and so shall we ever be with the Lord" (I Thessalonians 4:17).

But with the current emergence of the new breed of apostles and prophets, false doctrines like those refuted by the apostle Paul in Thessalonica have become established. It is the antithesis of biblical doctrine regarding the future rapture of the church

While Paul's correction exposed the false teaching that Christ had already returned (see II Thessalonians 2:1-2), our day sees a vehement denial of Paul's teaching on the rapture. An incident at New Covenant highlighted these teachings about a year and a half before my family and I left.

Cleaning up after the Sunday service, my conversation with one of our members took an unexpected turn. My mention of the rapture produced an interesting response: "I'm not sure it's going to happen," the sister said with some conviction.

Taken aback, I said, "But what about the passage in I Thessalonians? It says the Lord Himself will descend from heaven with a shout and we'll be taken up to be with Him."

"Well," she responded in an offhand way, "there are a lot of different interpretations of that Scripture." With a smile she added, "Personally, I'm a pan-tribulationist. No matter what happens, I believe it will all pan out."

This may be a clever sounding phrase, but it is hardly sound doctrine. I was thoroughly flustered by the conversation's end and approached Tom Smalley, who was putting away the sound equipment. When I explained what had just transpired, he smiled wryly, nodded, and informed me that he was aware of this sister's strange belief. But since he reckoned he and she had already had one verbal conflict too many (there was a control issue that affected them both), he would not attempt to correct her. After Tom's departure, she evidently felt free to teach this same belief to a weaker member of our group who came to one home fellowship confused.

I can see now where the sister in New Covenant may have been exposed to it. Another doctrinal group, the Manifest Sons of God, took the Latter Rain collage of teaching a dramatic step further, focusing on a particular, out-of-context verse in the book of Romans that seemed to promise them incredible transformation: "For the earnest expectation of the creature waiteth for the manifestation of the sons of God" (Romans 8:19).

In context, this verse actually speaks of the redemption and transformation of our physical bodies at Christ's return. However, Manifest Sons doctrine teaches that this Scripture is a promise of *present* transformation, that we may have spiritual bodies like the resurrected Christ. The idea is that, if Christians would live holy enough, some would eventually reach a state of sinless perfection, which would result in "present immortality." Though the Assemblies of God tried to correct this faulty interpretation through its condemnation of Manifest Sons teaching in 1949, this belief is alive and well in some charismatic groups.

The traditional view of the rapture is very threatening to people of the Manifest Sons mindset. If Christ was to return before the physical body took on incorruptibility, or before the church rose up to claim the kingdoms of this world for God, it would be a signal defeat to those who had struggled so hard in their own efforts.

The Headwaters of the River

The Manifest Sons of God is an extremist group that was birthed from what became known as the Latter Rain movement. In February of 1948 in North Battleford, Saskatchewan, a community of believers met to seek God for His power. A power did manifest. Miracles were reported, and Christians from all over set out on a pilgrimage to get this power. The Latter Rain movement emerged full-blown, evidencing supposed signs and wonders, prophetic utterances, and impartations via the laying on of hands. The movement was also marked with a spirit of elitism, false prophecies, and an inbred authority structure based upon the new "word of the Lord." When the Christian community was faced with the decision between solid biblical teaching and awe-inspiring miracles, many swung their legs over the fence of indecision and jumped with both feet into one of the first major 20th century tributaries of the River. The reasoning went that a *new thing*, based on the prophecy in Isaiah 43:18-19, had sprung up. All concerns about doctrine or practice could be dealt with sometime down the road, if at all. The pendulum had swung from the Word to experience as the final arbiter.

What many do not realize is that two issues factored heavily into this revival. The first is that a 1946 book written by Franklin Hall, called *Atomic Power with God Through Fasting and Prayer*,[10] was read and promoted by the revival's leaders. The other is that one of the foremost prophets of the era, William Branham, had imparted his ministry power through the laying on of hands to some of those involved in this revival. His teachings were a strong determining factor in the Saskatchewan revival's course.

The Franklin Hall book is a strong call to return the church to a pattern of fasting and prayer. While the premise of fasting is itself biblical, the book strangely asserted that without the *discipline* of fasting, prayer goes unanswered. As *proof*, Hall even cites the answered prayer received by pagans offering supplications to their false gods. In his excellent analysis of Dominion doctrine and practice, *Vengeance Is Ours: The Church in Dominion,* noted Christian researcher Al Dager astutely observes:

> If we analyze Hall's claims, we must come to the conclusion that those who pray to demons will have their prayers answered if they fast, but Christians will not have their prayers answered if they don't fast. At the least, it seems, they would be hindered greatly.[11]

In another of Hall's books, he wrote that the church would eventually produce an elite group of overcomers with the power to defy the laws of gravity, to walk upside down, and even attain to present immortality. He also spoke of a shining gold dust appearing on the skin of believers. Interesting that reports of this kind of phenomena have been circulating in River churches—even though at least one chemically-analyzed "gold dust" sample proved to be nothing more than children's plastic glitter.[12]

William Branham, called by some in today's prophetic ministries the greatest prophet to have ever lived, had also drunk deeply of Hall's teachings, including *Atomic Power with God Through Fasting and Prayer.* Emerging into the late 1940s spotlight with a reputation for accurate words of knowledge and miraculous healing power, Branham astounded the multitudes. It was said he could tell a person he'd never before met what conversations the person had and the situation which he was facing, and he could speak restoration to a chronically diseased part of the body and heal it. He made it known that he was a prophet of the Lord, and his preaching drew the crowds. But what those same crowds didn't generally hear were some of his other pet doctrines.

Branham taught that Satan had sex with Eve in the Garden of Eden, and Cain was the result of that union. He taught that he himself was the seventh angel of the book of Revelation, that he was Elijah the prophet, and that a belief in the Trinity was of the devil. But as long as he kept these beliefs under his hat and continued to wow the mob, the invitations to speak at churches worldwide kept pouring in.

His life certainly appeared marked by the miraculous. And Branham had no hesitation to say so. His testimony included a halo around him at his birth, and an actual photo of him in later life shows what appears to be a ring of light around his head while he stands at the pulpit preaching. It's what his followers have sometimes called The Pillar of Fire. This strange phenomenon supposedly happened in grander manifestation on June 11, 1933 as Branham was baptizing converts in the Ohio River near Jefferson, Indiana. Hearing a *voice* tell him to look up, Branham beheld a mysterious, star-like light in the sky, which rapidly descended until it rested just above him. Some in the crowd of 4,000 fell in worship, others ran in terror. The voice commissioned Branham, telling him that as John the Baptist was the forerunner of the Messiah, so Branham would be the forerunner of Christ's second coming.

On February 28, 1963 a few miles from Tucson, Arizona, an immense, bright ring of cloud appeared in the clear sky. Branham claimed he was caught up into its midst where it turned out to be "seven mighty angels" who had appeared to give him yet another divine commission; this time he was to make known to the church the mystery of the seven seals of the book of Revelation.[13]

Taken at face value, this means that the incomplete church had waited two thousand years for Branham to appear on the scene.

A presence made itself known around Branham throughout his life. He had been followed since childhood by a spiritual being that, when Branham reached manhood, manifested as a young man with long hair and flowing robes. Stepping out from a ball of brilliant light, this being commissioned him to go out and heal the afflicted and said that he would know of diseases present that affected an individual by vibrations in his left hand. Branham also claimed to have been given another spiritual gift—he would know what was in the hearts of men.[14]

Killed by injuries received in an automobile collision in 1965, Branham has physically faded from the scene, but his legacy of incredible tales, supernatural signs, and *prophetic anointing* lives on. He has a following to this day.

Branham's tradition of sensing the anointing in one's hands is something that continues as well. Many of those within the old Latter Rain ranks, and in the Faith Movement that followed, claim heat or vibrations in their hands which they believe indicates the presence of God for healing. New Covenant Fellowship was no different. Anyone in our group with a sudden feeling of hot hands could ask for a halt to the Sunday service in order to minister with the laying on of hands.

While Branham and Latter Rain proponents claimed allegiance to God's inerrant Word, their practices and peculiar doctrines denied it. Here are some of the basic beliefs they do adhere to:

- A great, end-times army will arise and take authority over the earth, putting Satan and his minions under their feet.

- The last days remnant of the true church (meaning those adhering to the Latter Rain doctrine) are the elite.

- Specific desirable anointings can be imparted from person to person by the laying on of hands.

- The church needs to experience *restoration* of all the gifts and revelation knowledge of who we really are in order to walk in fullness of power and finally be complete.

- Modern apostles and prophets must be set up in the church and the elect must submit to them.

- Restoration of the five-fold ministry of Ephesians 4:11 must take place for that authority structure to be erected.

- The church must come into complete physical unity.

- The rapture of believers is a myth, spawned by Satan to corral the church into a retreat mentality.

Some Latter Rain adherents no longer wait with yearning for the redemption of our bodies at the Second Coming. Now, in place of the rapture, they teach to expect Christ to come *in* us, instead of *for* us.

According to the Bible, believers in the last days are not, in triumph, going to make the nations fall at their feet (Matthew 24:9). And as for the need for restoration of revelation knowledge in order to be complete—we've always been complete in Christ Jesus (Colossians 2:10). We have always had all the authority (Matthew 28:18; Titus 2:11-15), gifts, and revelation knowledge needed to live righteous before Him and be witnesses of Christ before a lost world (II Peter 1:3). This last point is one of most damaging evidences against the Latter Rain movement. If, as proponents insist, a new outpouring of the Holy Spirit is necessary for the completion of the church, then at some point in world history, the outpouring of the Spirit that began on the day of Pentecost was no longer effective. In other words, there was not enough of the Holy Spirit to carry over into the 21st century. Talk about putting God in a box! The God of the Bible is big enough to carry on the work of the Spirit's empowering throughout world history. He doesn't need to create it over and over, as Latter Rain doctrine insists.

As for the need for modern apostles and prophets, if what we are presently seeing in the church is the best the Latter Rain can produce … well, that calls into question the basic premise of the movement itself. The apostles of the New Testament along with the Old Testament prophets have already built the foundation and framework. The canon of Scripture is forever closed. Prophets, by their pronouncements, add to the Bible. This was their purpose before the complete written testimony was set down. There is nothing lacking in the scriptural record. Today's supposed prophets add to the Bible. While they vehemently deny this, a quick glance at their *words from the Lord* is enough evidence to stop them cold. Rick Joyner's Jesus either is or isn't the God of the Scriptures. If He is, then it is incumbent upon us to act upon every word uttered by Him. If He is not, then what Joyner saw in his dream/vision was false, a deceiving spirit, or the product of Joyner's own mind. For Joyner to say with finality *the Lord said*, as he does in *The Final Quest* and *The Call*, is to equate his own writings with Scripture. After all, what is Scripture but the words of God—and as God, Jesus spoke the very Word of God.

The Old *New Thing*

It is impossible to understand the current River phenomenon outside its proper context. The teachings and practices characterizing this movement go back long before the events of the North Battleford revival. Indeed, what has been billed from the 1940s onward as the New Thing is yellowed with age. The average, modern hyper-charismatic churchgoer has a rather restricted view of church history. This common weakness allowed the bizarre manifestations and doctrines to flourish at New Covenant Fellowship and to determine our entire spiritual outlook. The same is happening in an alarming number of church groups worldwide.

The term *latter rain* has been in use at least since the late 1890s. During the last half of the 19th Century, a fervent desire for revival ran high in many Christian groups. Spurred on by the teachings of A.B. Simpson, Dwight L. Moody, and R. A. Torrey, expectation grew for a return to New Testament (miraculous) power and the working of the gifts of the Spirit within the congregational setting. Several Holiness sects also preached a form of sinless perfection, a doctrine that surprisingly hearkens back to John and Charles Wesley and the Great Awakening; some of the resultant groups hung onto this doctrine like a lifeline. There was also the development of a belief that a return to a *primitive* Christianity would mark a climactic ingathering of lost souls at the end of the age. This yearning drove many to heartfelt prayer. It was believed the Second Coming was only a breath away, preceded by the catching up of the saints in a secret rapture, and the manifestation of signs and wonders was eagerly looked for in anticipation of these events.

Many in the Pentecostal/charismatic camp speak of the Latter Rain as if it's a fresh-faced theological newcomer. But the students at North Battleford didn't coin its use. More than a decade earlier, Aimee Semple McPherson was speaking about the *latter rain* that would fall on the church's faithful. As early as the late 1890s, congregations were waiting for the downpour of the latter rain that would usher in the great end-times revival with signs and wonders.

Does any of this sound familiar?

Most Pentecostals today trace their origins to the Azusa Street revival of 1906. But Azusa was not birthed in a vacuum. Among other things, it was spurred in part by the ministries of two men—Frank W. Sandford and Charles Fox Parham.

Sandford had built an impressive complex of buildings near Durham, Maine, which he called Shiloh. Many who had fallen under the influence of his charismatic leadership came to live on the site, working incessantly on its additions and engaging in regular, intensive prayer and fasting while tending the kitchen, grounds, or hospital.

Sandford forbade his people to receive medical treatment for any sickness, and the community weathered outbreaks of smallpox, diphtheria, and tuberculosis, battling these illnesses with the prayer of faith. Many passed away because of his anti-medicine edict, preferring death to disobedience to their leader. His hospital was more for faith healing and prayer than it was for actual medical treatment.[15]

Sandford's life was guided by a voice which proclaimed him to be Elijah the prophet, the forerunner of the Second Coming of Christ. A restorationist, he set out to bring the kingdom of God to earth, traveling the world in his personal yacht to many countries and pronouncing their inhabitants free of the bondage of Satan. Sandford declared both himself and a close associate at Shiloh, Charles Holland, to be the Two Witnesses of the book of Revelation, destined to be martyred on the streets of Jerusalem.[16] He had a propensity to baptize converts in midwinter lakes, having chopped through the thick ice, and at least one sixty-eight year old woman died from pneumonia due to the immersion. For years his people at Shiloh came near to starvation while he and his family always seemed to have plenty to eat. Sandford was eventually indicted on manslaughter charges for the deaths of six people under his direct supervision, who died of scurvy and malnutrition aboard his yacht. For months they had helped him evade capture by the U.S. Coast Guard, which was trying to serve him an outstanding warrant. He was sentenced to ten years in prison.

Like our modern *prophets,* Sandford demanded immediate obedience to his whims and condemned to hell fire those who rebelled. His prophecies fell flat with ho-hum regularity even as he amazingly declared them fulfilled. Neither he nor Charles Holland died on the streets of Jerusalem. Sandford, who died many years ago, has a following yet today.

Charles Fox Parham spent time ministering with Sandford and admired him, taking the idea for his own Bethel Bible School in Topeka, Kansas, from Sandford's own *Holy Ghost and Us* facility. Like Sandford, Parham was a firm adherent of Anglo-Israelism, the belief that the ten lost tribes of Israel went to Great Britain and from there to the United States. This belief naturally made white Anglo-Saxons the descendants of the biblical tribes and hence superior to other people groups. Parham believed that the Baptism of the Holy Spirit sealed the Bride of Christ (what he believed was the 144,000 who had come out from the institutional church), and kept them from the destruction of the plagues prophesied in the book of Revelation. He also rejected the concept of a literal hell in favor of God's annihilation of the unbeliever.

Although by his own admission Parham surrendered his participation in Freemasonry when he began his ministry, he nonetheless thought highly enough of it to present a gavel to a Masonic lodge in Wichita years after he began his ministry.[17] Writing about one of his later visits to the Azusa Street revival he speaks in racial epithets of the mix of white and black worshippers, and in his later years he showed sympathies towards the Ku Klux Klan.[18]

In the rush to head to the current *revivals*, many in the church look past the historical record of the real thing. There are many instances of true revivals in the Bible—Ezra 10, Nehemiah 8, II Kings 23:1-24, and of course the book of Acts, an account of one revival after another, both small and great. The manifestations that occurred in converts during this ever-continuing move of God were identical: fear of the Lord, heart repentance that included weeping over sins, destroying objects of witchcraft or idol worship, great joy, a love for the fellowship of other Christians, a hunger for the Word of God. While these true revivals did not have spiritual drunkenness, holy laughter, etc., I'd venture to say that the holy attitude of those early saints far outshines anything we see in today's River-style revivals.

A Little Seasoning, Please

It is impossible to overestimate the damage done to the body of Christ by both Latter Rain and John Wimber's doctrine of self-validating experience. Having begun under Jason Klein in the Word of Faith heresy, we at New Covenant Fellowship naturally progressed through Tom Smalley's aggressive leadership into the paradigm shift of Wimber's Vineyard Movement, and from there into the explosive deceptions of the Toronto Blessing and the Brownsville Revival. It reached such a fever pitch in both doctrine and the pursuit of the *power* that it wasn't until I stepped back and observed the situation from a genuine biblical perspective that the picture as God would see it began to emerge.

I finally came to the point of believing that a *different Jesus* had been presented to our congregation, along with a whole new variety of anointings, methods, practices, and ideas that absolutely could not be supported by Scripture. In fact, I'd have to say it had always been so. Now, please don't misunderstand. The atonement of the Cross, forgiveness through the blood of Christ, the deity of Jesus, the Trinity—all these things were taught, of course. But the additions and the interpretations, many of which altered the very character and nature of God, were also taught and, more practically, adhered to. With the Latter Rain and the new thing trumpeted by its globe-trotting prophets, it was officially declared in our group that the sky was the limit.

Even before I took a public stand against these doctrines, I found they all grew boring with time. I began every Sunday looking forward to the service, hungry for genuine worship and the taste of the Word of God, and almost without fail our last three years at New Covenant brought recurring frustration and emptiness. It became increasingly difficult to endure the worship part of the service, with its pomp and hype, and I'd find myself wandering throughout the building or standing outside for a quarter of an hour just to escape. The sermons at times nearly lulled me to sleep, and I'd find my mind wandering to questions, questions. Our meetings had become a place of internment, and even as I was frustrated that the manifestations didn't occur with me, conversely I was irritated they seemed so contrived.

The taste of our doctrine had become fouled and polluted, yet we were so mesmerized by the manifestations and super-power teachings that we didn't even recognize it. It reminded me of my teenage years in Philadelphia, fishing in the historic Delaware River. Whatever I caught—catfish, perch, carp—I knew I had to throw it back because it was too dangerous to eat. That wide, beautiful river carried enough industrial waste to take out a herd of elephants. Anything that managed to eke out an existence in its tawdry waters carried the same poison in its bloodstream. No amount of holding our noses and faking its delicacy could give fish caught there a better flavor or content. It's high time we stop kidding ourselves. For all the elitism and magnified spirituality we're supposed to exhibit, much of the modern church has grown tasteless. The so-called revival has done little to effect surrounding communities—crime is still skyrocketing, practical atheism is rampant, and, even among Christians the knowledge of God is whatever anyone wants it to be. This movement as a whole has produced an elitist group that proclaims itself enlightened, while deriding the Scriptures that speak of certain judgment for such behaviors and beliefs:

> For the time will come when they will not endure sound doctrine; but after their own lusts shall they heap to themselves teachers, having itching ears; And they shall turn away their ears from the truth, and shall be turned unto fables. (II Timothy 4:3-4)

CHAPTER 11

DOUBTS

"Anything that cannot be found in Scripture
has to be rejected outright—totally rejected."

There. David Wilkerson had said what I'd been feeling for a very long time. I stared at the words with a profound sense of fear, confusion, and just a trace of hope.

The October 1999 issue of *Charisma* magazine lay open with the side-by-side faces of David Wilkerson and Rodney Howard-Browne staring up at me. I went through the article several times. Even the title, "David Wilkerson Blasts Faith Preachers in Sermon," was riveting, and I read it over and over. I'm not absolutely certain why. Perhaps to make sure it was real. Here was someone I knew and trusted, a man of God whose career I had followed closely for nearly ten years, and he was speaking words to my heart that no one had ever dared. He was putting voice to suspicions I'd had for years, clothing them with apt descriptions and making them frighteningly tangible.

Wilkerson, pastor of Times Square Church in New York City, in his sermon of April 11th that year, "The Reproach of the Solemn Assembly," called the leaders of the Word of Faith movement to account.[1] One by one he went over various issues regarding the heresies preached by Kenneth Hagin, Kenneth Copeland, and, without mentioning him by name, Benny Hinn. He encouraged those of his flock in possession of Word of Faith literature to burn it; warned them to stay away from Rodney Howard-Browne's July 7-August 14

"Good News New York" crusade; and exploded the myth of God's moving in the River, with its manifestations of wild laughing, drunk in the spirit, and animal posturing. He roundly condemned them all, even citing a Word of Faith conference where one of the speakers bragged about his $15,000 dog and $32,000 ring.

In that moment a door opened into a very dark room. It was just a crack, letting in barely enough light to let me know I didn't like what it revealed. But, for the first time, I put aside my charismatic programming and decided to take a closer look. I figured if someone of Wilkerson's caliber—famous but honest, humble, and with a holy hatred for sin—came out in the open about these issues then maybe, just maybe it would be okay for me to do so as well. What gave me courage was the fact that he had violated the unwritten law of the hyper-charismatic—don't name names. He had done just that, and repeatedly, disdaining the repercussions he would so obviously reap. While I do not agree with the exegesis of some of Wilkerson's sermons, I knew he would not lightly condemn a man or ministry.

Having just arrived home from Sunday afternoon service and after nearly memorizing the article, I did something completely out of routine for me—I headed for the computer and clicked onto the Internet. Typing "laughing revival" in the search box, I whizzed off into cyberspace … and entered a world I hadn't known existed.

Here it was, right before me. One right after another. Article after article critiquing holy laughter, drunk in the spirit, and God's Bartender. Some of the material was a bit on the accusing side, with little biblical support. These I avoided. But the majority was well written and presented solid scriptural evidence. I focused on discourses given by Pentecostal ministers; I felt that if the time came for me to present my findings to New Covenant leadership, they might more readily accept what I had to share if it came from like-minded sources.

Suspicions took solid form, and as the truth grabbed me by the shirtfront and gave me a hard shake, I got just plain mad.

Running some copies off the printer, I took them to Kris some time later as she sat at the kitchen table. "Look at this," I said excitedly. "You won't believe what I found out."

As I began to read some of the material out loud it became painfully obvious that Kris didn't share my outrage. Listening at first, she then grew impatient and offered a few comments (I believe out of sheer confusion) to the effect that I should calm down and make sure I had gotten my facts straight.

Maybe she was right, I thought, but having gotten my foot in the door, I wasn't about to let it slam shut again without a fight.

The computer at once became my staunch ally and a massive stumbling block between my wife and me. Most other interests dropped away, and I spent hours a day on the Internet, blocking incoming phone calls and frustrating Kris' own efforts to contact me when she was out of the house. Completely out of character, I began keeping late nights. I couldn't have stopped if I'd wanted to, not if I wanted a clean conscience. I was driven to know, no matter what it cost.

And cost it would.

Passing the Baton

Tom Smalley had left the pastorate about two months earlier to move to the east coast. Before leaving, he appointed Phil Clayton as New Covenant Fellowship's pastor, encouraging him to apply for his minister's license with a larger church that our congregation had been part of for about two years. Phil did this, and it seemed we were on our way.

At first, it appeared Phil was the shot in the arm the flock needed. The first Sunday he took the pulpit he told us that as a working man with a sizable family to support, he didn't have time to do everything expected of a traditional pastor. While accepting the duties of pastor, Phil reminded the congregation that it was our responsibility to move into the things of the God. He took a firm stand, and I was both proud and supportive of him. In the leadership meeting just prior to the service, the elders along with their wives had committed themselves to aid Phil in any way needed, recognizing his headship and promising to stand with him. Dale Lewis, one of our overseers who was in the position of what could be termed an area supervisor, had presented all of us with the mandate that we would have to recognize Phil's vision for New Covenant Fellowship and submit to it. As Dale noted, "The buck stops here."

It appeared that Phil might be open to addressing some of the doctrinal errors that had long been preached within our congregation.

Teacher, I Have a Question...

What should someone do who has found himself becoming (perhaps involuntarily) enlightened? I mention involuntarily, for it is often that way. God in His mercy continues to reach out with the illumination of both His Spirit and His Word, only we often don't recognize His voice if it goes against prior training. The person shuts out the warnings, those little nudges in his own spirit that signal danger, believing his leaders to be spiritually superior and not wanting to come out from under the *covering* of church authority. Plus, as strange as it may seem, there is often a dread of the truth, and many people simply cannot tolerate it. Consider it this way—if you've been a Christian for any number of years, have submitted to doctrines that puffed up your pride or offered a veneer of spiritual maturity, if you've been slain in the spirit dozens of times, had visions, dreams or given prophecies, *and* have taught others to accept the same criteria of spirituality … well, you've got a lot of repenting to do, both before the Lord in private and publicly if you've been teaching in an official capacity. It can be very humbling and scary to stand before people who have hung on your every word and looked to you for guidance and admit to gross error.

Standing at a fork in the road, there are only two ways to go, and the path with the least bumps seems quite appealing at that moment.

For myself, there was only a brief hesitation, possibly because my *rebellious* nature had long before provoked me to read material (like *The Seduction of Christianity*) considered anathema to most mainstream charismatics. I had already gotten in the habit of asking troubling questions and confronting leadership over confusing issues. Many were the times Tom and I locked horns over some doctrinal issue, and although he always secured a surface victory, my mental file cabinet of unanswered questions grew.

The bottom line for facing discovery of the false is—what will you do with the truth? We cannot have it both ways. Something is either true or it is not. If what we believe is of God, then we are bound to live by it. Anything less would be rebellion. For years, I wandered in the thick, smothering fog of the gray zone, or areas of uncertainty. Having been exposed to the harsh black-and-white of Tom's prophetic ministry (an attitude of "This is the way it is and you'll just have to get used to it!"), I wanted no part of condemning either my own or others' beliefs, and found it very uncomfortable to take a hard-line stance on anything. Oddly, I had acquired this very trait under the pastors who roundly condemned sin from the pulpit, but didn't recognize the sin of false doctrine in their own lives.

And sin it is: monstrous, consuming, supplanting the true knowledge of God with an unsatisfying counterfeit, false doctrine will eventually devour a person's conscience, so that he thinks right is wrong and day is night:

> Woe unto them that call evil good, and good evil; that put darkness for light, and light for darkness; that put bitter for sweet, and sweet for bitter! (Isaiah 5:20)

When our eyes finally begin to open we must not turn away, no matter how great the temptation to do so. Would we despise the grace of God, who in lovingkindness and forbearance has put up with our awful disobedience for so long? No matter what you've been taught, the door will not remain open indefinitely. In this sensual, mystical "revival," we can become like those whose conscience is seared (I Timothy 4:1-2). Doctrines of demons always lead us to a different image of the Godhead.

What should you do when a question comes up about doctrine, practice, or fellowship? What the Bereans did makes good sense, and they were commended in the pages of Scripture for their decision:

> These were more noble than those in Thessalonica, in that they received the word with all readiness of mind, and searched the scriptures daily, whether those things were so. (Acts 17:11)

In the Greek, the word searched means to investigate, scrutinize, ask questions, or put on trial. This is what we need to do with every doctrine brought into the congregational arena. In fact, Paul commanded the Corinthian believers to do this very thing (I Corinthians 10:15). When I finally began doing this on a personal level, I was struck with horror. What had I done? I had taught these doctrines to believers, publicly fought for them, practiced them. I had walked in the power myself at times. And I was looked up to. The whole idea of status in our congregation began crumbling. I was broken before God, and I let it sink in—I didn't want to escape the shock of realization. In esteeming false teachers and promoting deception, I had greatly dishonored the Lord and had turned the corner into that which I most hated. With heartfelt repentance, I was determined to do a complete about-face.

Into the Fray

After the initial two weeks of preliminary research, I enthusiastically approached Pastor Phil about the prophetic movement worldwide, and in particular how it was practiced in our group. I felt hopeful that he would be receptive and even welcome my findings. Preparing a one-page statement documenting some of the basic flaws in the material our group had been reading (including Rick Joyner's *The Final Quest*), I emailed the paper to him. I phoned him later in the week, set up a time two weeks following to meet and present some material firsthand, and settled back into a routine of "search and document."

Due probably to an amateur historian's love for accurate dates and descriptions, and aided by my ongoing stint as a minor-league journalist with one of our local newspapers, I focused on validating fraudulent doctrine by words out of the preachers' own mouths and public practices that were part of their ministries. For instance, Bob Jones' teaching about his color-changing hands was a matter of record, documented in the 1989 audio tape *Visions and Revelations* with Mike Bickle. Therefore, I would use it as part of my presentation. I had also previously dropped off at Phil's home a small packet of maybe fifteen pages of evidence to verify the accuracy of my concerns.

When I showed up at Pastor Phil's home on the appointed day, he met me at the door with a surprised expression, having forgotten we were to meet at all. On his way out the door to his son's softball game, he promised to set aside time the following week. Deflated, I left with the stack of material I had brought along, confused that such a congregational dilemma did not warrant immediate concern from our shepherd.

When the meeting did finally take place, it was a perplexing waste of time. Despite his having some of the material in his possession for weeks, Phil had yet to go through the little I had given him to read, and was therefore unprepared to field specific questions. His attitude baffled me; he was calm, reserved and unhurried, and sure didn't show any signs of being concerned or alarmed over what I had discovered. With Kris sitting beside me at the Clayton's kitchen table, I weathered nearly a half-hour of preliminary condescension and subtle mockery from Beth, who seemed to view my concerns as no more than the British proverbial "tempest in a teacup." Her insinuations against my biblical understanding at one point made me feel nearly nauseous, and in a silent whirl of emotion I nearly got up and walked out. After a while she calmed down, eased up on the throttle, and both of them assured us they would look more closely at these concerns.

While Kris was hopeful because they had at least partially heard us out, I felt discouraged. Why had we not even opened our Bibles to check on the validity of both our practices and those of the teachers from whom we received training materials? And I was puzzled why these two people whom I had so trusted did not seem at all alarmed at what was going on. Initially encouraged by Phil's transition to the pulpit, I began to feel very uneasy, with doubts I didn't know were there flooding me. In the months to follow, I would find out just how hard it would be to swim against the flow of the River's sweeping current.

Why the Resistance?

One of the most frustrating aspects of confronting these difficult issues was the resistance I encountered if I even so much as raised a question. Something I quickly discovered was that once a congregation is afloat on this raging torrent of mystical experience and self-glorifying doctrine, nobody wants to rock the boat. It is much easier to allow oneself to be carried along to the next manifestation or high-powered teaching, and to absolve oneself of responsibility. Nobody likes to be told he or she is wrong, and concerning things of such a powerful, subjective nature as this Third Wave, it is especially difficult to convince people of faulty reasoning or abandonment of Scripture. We were taught that to question is basically equivalent to calling a work of God Satan's work. It is considered equivalent to the religious leaders of his day accusing Jesus of casting out demons by Beelzebub, the prince of demons.

Teachers themselves are particularly hard to reach, since they have pounded their message home time and again with their authority as shepherds of God's flock. They have coaxed and at times threatened their congregations into compliance with un-biblical manifestations and beliefs, and have made public spectacles of themselves by getting slain in the spirit, having demons cast out of them, or laughing uncontrollably for hours on end at nothing at all. Their hard-won reputations in certain circles would suffer irreparable damage if they were to admit to being a fountain of false doctrine and by so doing incriminate co-leaders in the ministry. They would also have to come clean with the fact that much of the congregation's tithe money over the years was utilized to fund projects promoting false teachers, flooding the group with heretical materials, and jetting the pastor to nationwide conferences hosting what is fraudulent.

Faced with these frightening consequences, not many pastors, teachers, or elders are willing to step into the light, ask forgiveness, and, if necessary, step down from the pulpit. The stakes are just too high.

Torn Apart

As my research progressed, a shower of pieces began to fill the gaping holes in the puzzle of New Covenant Fellowship's teachings. At times I nearly laughed at the ridiculous hilarity of it all; other times I wept, repented, and feared. When Phil saw the situation was not just going to go away, he asked where I was heading with it. I told him I didn't know, but deep inside I was beginning to see what was coming with frightening clarity. My role as elder was hanging in the balance. Eldership loomed large before me, and the respectability afforded, but the way things were going I knew it couldn't last. It was only a matter of time until I formally stepped down.

Phil flatly refused to go public, insisting that all my concerns were only a matter of private interpretation. He could see things in a different light, he said, and saw no point in exposing a brother from the pulpit, even if consistent heresy was present in the man's ministry. Consulting with the overseer provided by our larger church connection, Dale Lewis, Phil was encouraged to proceed with great caution, and this because Dale believed the Toronto Blessing to be of God. At New Covenant the previous summer, Dale had ministered the gold teeth anointing a la Toronto. Skeptical, but not wanting to hinder God, I had stood, along with the entire congregation, as Dale prayed for our standard amalgam tooth fillings to be transformed. No flashlights were necessary for the characteristic peek into the mouth. No one's teeth manifested any change whatsoever. But Dale's faithfulness to the Toronto power was unwavering, and his counsel to Phil was received and acted upon.

When I confronted Phil about Toronto preacher Wes Campbell's traveling Braveheart anointing, which requires him to outfit in full Scottish Highland regalia when preaching to some congregations, Phil could not fault the man's performance. And performance it was. Taken from the R-rated movie that was littered with obscenity and drenched in gore, Campbell's impersonation should never have had place in any church service.

An e-mail I received from Philip Powell in Australia echoed my own aversion to Campbell's portrayal. The National General

Secretary of the Assemblies of God in Australia from 1989-1992, Powell resigned his post after a lonely and valiant fight for the integrity of the Scriptures amidst a barrage of false teaching entering into the Assemblies' ranks. He continues the same stand in opposition to the current River movement and the flood of false teachers who have gained acceptance in mainstream Christianity. Powell is currently the director of Christian Witness Ministries, a worldwide outreach alerting the church to aberrant doctrines and exposing those who preach them. In correspondence to me, Powell stated:

> Wesley Campbell was featured on a video preaching at a large Assembly of God Church in Garden City Brisbane (Australia).... On the video Mr. Campbell mimicked the actor who played the lead part in the film called *Braveheart*. His face had been painted in blue and white stripes just as in the film. My wife and I decided to rent *Braveheart* to see what the film was all about. We were shocked and couldn't watch most of it. The violence was the worst I had ever seen.... We particularly wanted to hear the speech on which it was claimed Wes Campbell had based his message, which he has allegedly preached all over the world. The speech in the secular film contained outrageous obscenities. We were shocked and offended.

All of that was unimportant to Phil Clayton. He cited precedent in the Foursquare Church founder, Aimee Semple McPherson. Her stage theatrics in preaching the Gospel drew tremendous crowds.

Phil rejected nearly everything I had to say. I believe he was scared and confused. Having been indoctrinated into acceptance of all these bizarre doctrines, critical examination had never entered his mind. He once admitted that he had made promises to me he didn't keep, and he had put me off because of the discomfort I was bringing into his personal sphere.

All this left me in an extremely delicate and painful position. Knowing what needed to be done, I was caught between my love for Phil and desire to submit to his directives and my growing love for the truth. Phil, and in fact the entire New Covenant leadership was pulling me one way, the Scriptures and the Spirit of God another.

Meanwhile, a brutal toll was being exacted on my home life. Kris and I could not discuss the issues without heated argument. Agreeing with some of my research, but convinced of the good intentions of two people she greatly loved (Phil and Beth Clayton), she believed me too harsh and accusing, and attempted to bargain for more patience on my part. At times I *was* harsh, and became progressively so for the first few months, but only because of the blasé attitude demonstrated by my pastor and the rest of the leadership. If I was so wrong, why didn't we all just meet as a body and openly discuss what I had been presenting? That would give them ample opportunity to refute the evidence.

Lessons From Those Who Stood

It seemed nearly every waking moment was concentrated on exploring biblical practice, solidifying evidence, and transcribing correlative documentation. The strain began to show physically. Often I'd lie awake at night and stare at the dark ceiling, fear gnawing at me. Was I doing the right thing? Who in the world did I think I was? Did the reservoir of truth reside in me alone, and were all others in New Covenant Fellowship in error?

On the Internet I had been reading about others in the same situation as I, and corresponded with many of them. I belonged to a group who posted on a discernment website, and I grew to know the pain of others caught in the same intractable web. Many of them had paid a dear price within their churches and their families when they stood against false doctrine. The stories I heard became my inspiration to do the same regardless of the cost. As an ex-Catholic, I had long admired many of the early reformers who took heroic stands against the Church of Rome. I prayed and hoped I could do the same in far less dire circumstances than they had faced during inquisitions and torturous deaths.

As further confirmation, two of our close friends, Robert and Jill Anderson, had been doing their own inquiring into the Scriptures after two months of dialogue with me, and they too had been posing some difficult questions to Phil for a period of months. One three-hour meeting in the church office convinced them of the futility of further discussion. Phil was not going to change his position, and they knew it. His refusal to publicly discuss specific false doctrines and name those who promoted them presented a brick wall to their trust in him as their shepherd.

They left New Covenant Fellowship that week.

"Touch Not Mine Anointed"

Perhaps the single biggest factor hindering acknowledgment and genuine repentance of false doctrine is the unwillingness for believers to relinquish the superstar status of their spiritual heroes. And how many times had our leadership supported this by telling us not to name names? It was the one thing above all others that tied my hands and put a gag in my mouth. Although Phil told me to go ahead and speak to whomever I wanted to within our group, such presentations were always followed up with appropriate damage control by the leadership. And I was forbidden to breach the unwritten hyper-charismatic code and expose people like Kenneth Copeland during the times I filled the pulpit. The one time I did this, Beth Clayton later (in a meeting with Kris and me) scolded me for daring to broach the forbidden subject publicly before the congregation. This she did, despite the fact she had urged me three separate times prior to the sermon to "preach what God laid on your heart."

This fear of exposing God's anointed, even if they are guilty of repeated heresies, bordered on (may I use the term?) paranoia. Regardless of the evidence presented, there was simply no way anyone in our leadership would even admit the word heresy was applicable. Even when the blood atonement of Christ on the Cross is denied; even when those doing the denying are becoming rich through the tithes and offerings of believers who are often materially far worse off; even when these same ministers threaten divine judgment on those in opposition (the old Ananias and Sapphira tactic—Acts 5: 1-11).

Both the Old and New Testaments are replete with examples of the Lord's apostles and prophets condemning false brethren. Check out Ezekiel 34 sometime, plus the entire books of Isaiah and Jeremiah. Then look at Jesus' exposure of the hypocrisy and false teaching of His day, or the apostles' stern warnings in the epistles, such as found in the entire epistle of Jude. Anyone who claims the Bible commands silence on the subject simply doesn't know the Word as well as he thinks. Although false prophets are not stoned today (fortunate for them!), their sin will always be one of grave consequences.

> But though we, or an angel from heaven, preach any other gospel unto you than that which we have preached unto you, let him be accursed. As we said before, so say I now again, if any man preach any other gospel unto you than that ye have received, let him be accursed. (Galatians 1:8-9)

We must name them. How else will the church be warned? Would that we had the courage of a Nathan, to thunder with the righteous anger of the Almighty, "Thou art the man" (II Samuel 12:7)!

The false shepherds among us have too long used I Chronicles 16:22 and Psalm 105:15 as a blank check to do as they please. "Touch not mine anointed, and do my prophets no harm" was God's warning to the nations through which the Israelites passed during their sojourn through the wilderness. It implied swift judgment for any pagans who would come against the chosen people of the Lord. To wield this like a saber at a sincere brother alarmed at false doctrine smacks of spiritual tyranny, cowardice, and dishonesty. Hammered also with the Acts 5 account of the deaths of Ananias and Sapphira, a concerned believer in Jesus is usually bullied into silence or into leaving the congregation. It's already been used right here in our town to squelch close examination of extra-biblical manifestations.

While a big part of me just wanted out, Kris and I continued to hang on to a shredded hope for change, and we wound up staying months longer than we otherwise would have.

In the end, I'm glad we did. Had we left sooner, some nagging doubts may have remained in both our hearts, and could have become a wedge between us. New Covenant leadership, although not present in our home, would possibly have kept a foot in the door of our lives. So we settled down to wait, and what was hidden finally came full-blown into the light.

CHAPTER 12

Exit

"I am not prepared to say that Toronto is not of God, and that these animal manifestations are not of God. God is so much bigger than we can understand. God can do anything."

There you have it. In a nutshell, this is the mindset that the church of Jesus Christ is dealing with today. This remark from Beth Clayton, at a meeting in my home some months before my family and I left New Covenant Fellowship, encapsulates the corporate mentality of those teaching River theologies. Convinced that exposing serious error in the body of Christ belongs to God, they neglect or avoid the record of the Scriptures. Like all those before it, this particular meeting ended at an impasse. Only one avenue of dialogue remained, one which had been steadfastly resisted since day one—but one which should have been used at the first hint of danger.

A Gathering of Elders

Four couples sat in the Clayton's living room, eyes glued to the television set. Dramatic images of congregations moved by the power of the River created in us a variety of emotions. Personally, I felt gratification, a sense of finally having my day in court. It should never have taken a year to convene a meeting with such serious problems evident in both our own congregation and those in the church at large.

Images of spiritual drunkenness, men on all fours in manifestations of bulls and dogs, slain in the spirit phenomena that had men and women falling atop one another, one young man stiffening violently under the anointing and screaming as if in demon possession, another unable to even speak or stand erect by reason of the anointing … it went on and on.

When the fifteen-minute video segment ended, the official presentation began. Having brought along a packet of documentation, I placed it on the table before me and spoke of the contents. Here it was in black and white—teachers' own words, the bizarre unbiblical doctrines they promoted, the manifestations they initiated in their meetings. I should have realized I was in trouble when no one bothered to even seriously peruse the documentation.

Commenting on the video, a deacon's wife dryly noted, "We saw just what you wanted us to see." When pressed further, she declared that, since she had been in similar meetings, had seen changes for the better in others so touched, and had experienced such power herself, she knew it was of God, and nothing I could say would make any difference.

Although one of the leadership said that the video, "made my skin crawl," momentary reflection convinced him that, if done "decently and in order," animal manifestations might possibly be from the Spirit of God. Pastor Phil had concurred earlier with this perspective in a conversation with me, remarking that, "I can see there may be times when God could use animal manifestations to illustrate a scriptural truth or act out a message from Him."

This amazing viewpoint naturally poses a question—just *how* does a person bark "decently and in order"?

As far as even considering naming those preachers who promoted false doctrine within the entire leadership team—the idea itself was anathema. I suppose their reaction shouldn't have surprised me, having fought an uphill battle all the way, but I have to admit to some disappointment. Perhaps I believed that, in a group composed of so many New Covenant overseers and with such irrefutable evidence presented, at least one or two would have eyes to see the carnality for what it was. I was wrong. The meeting, though discussing some vague points about false doctrine and its propagators, never got around to addressing the issues, which had directed the spiritual course of our congregation for a dozen years. The bottom line seemed to be that because we each had experienced many of these same powerful manifestations ourselves, they simply had to be from God.

The only hopeful note came from one of the women present, who showed great surprise that Paul had publicly named two blasphemers, Hymenaeus and Alexander (1 Timothy 1:20). The rest of the meeting, however, was a bust. Although Pastor Phil set up the following week for a similar opportunity to study the issues, I began to see clearly what I was up against on a collective scale.

The Dreaded Word

Nearly everyone in our leadership cringed at the actual utterance of the word heresy. At its every mention, they regarded me with an alarmed expression that nearly yelled, "Don't say that!" and avoided the use of the term as if it were an unclean thing. Even presented with the Word of Faith doctrine that states the physical death of Christ on the Cross did not accomplish salvation, their heads would shake, mouths tighten, and hands would go up to bring a halt to further discussion.

It's as if it is considered unloving to bring serious departure from the Christian faith out into the light, and openly name the person involved. Interestingly, Paul had no such compunction (II Timothy 2:17-18), nor did the apostle John (3 John 9-10). Jesus called out the Pharisees to their face, in front of multitudes. We have the pattern set forth in the Word, but we simply refused to follow it, shrinking back behind an unbiblical definition of love.

What exactly is heresy? In II Peter 2:1, the word is used in the plural to indicate those who would bring in doctrines that contradict the Gospel set forth by our Lord and His apostles. In the Greek, the word—*hairesis*—comes from a word meaning "choice or opinion." Teachings contrary to the doctrine of Christ are built upon "imaginations, and every high thing that exalteth itself against the knowledge of God" (II Corinthians 10:5). They are the result of a minister's (or anyone's) personal choice to depart into another realm, "intruding into those things which he hath not seen, vainly puffed up by his fleshly mind" (Colossians 2:18). Heresies are mere opinions given a godly veneer, persuasive argument based upon assumptions, ideas, dreams, and visions not grounded in the revealed Word of God.

Heresy is not a light thing. In this relativistic, tolerant age, it is wrongly considered good manners to look the other way when someone expresses disagreement with objective truth. We have begun to find *common ground*, as some would put it, and link arms with Mormons and Muslims, believing the theological divide is not as wide as we had thought. Instead of bravely upholding the standard of scriptural inerrancy, we succumb to a redefinition of the very Gospel of our salvation which was once for all delivered unto the saints (Jude 3).

We have conveniently forgotten the martyrs who stood faithful to our Lord under penalty of death, who clung to the pure Word of God as the flames licked the soles of their bare feet, and the smoke of their own burning flesh seared their nostrils. We, who have never shed a drop of our own blood in defense of the Gospel, turn our backs upon those who have.

In the first of these eldership meetings, when I brought out the unwavering scriptural stance of the early reformers, one leader rebuked me and told me not to bring that up. I was stunned. Why not talk about our forefathers in the faith? If not for some of the early reformers, most of us would be Catholic. I remember well the feeling of being lost in a system of rules and superstition, and leaving the interpretation of Scripture to a clergy that sacrifices Christ again with every Mass. No, we must never forget or disparage the martyrs who "overcame him [the devil] by the blood of the Lamb, and by the word of their testimony; and they loved not their lives unto the death" (Revelation 12:11).

And yet, a new kind of Christian has taken the place of those earlier defenders of the faith. They have traded biblical Christianity for an experiential, mystical spirituality. Brothers and sisters, this shouldn't be! While there have always been *Christian* leaders and teachers who pervert the doctrine of Christ, we live in a time where there seems to be an increase of false doctrine permeating the halls of Christendom. We must not shy away from facing these heresies head-on.

Emancipation Proclamation

False doctrines and the practices that come with them do not set free— rather they enslave their adherents and hinder them from truly knowing God. This bondage was one of the main issues facing my wife and me upon examining the un-biblical doctrines we had been taught. As long as we believed the false, we were hemmed in on every side, backed into a corner by superstition and unbelief. Both of us having left one system of that ilk (Roman Catholicism), we had jumped feet first into another, and avoided the liberating message set forth in the Gospel. As with every religious system outside of the Gospel, do this, don't do that, don't touch, grab for this—a manmade set of rules had rendered the Word of God of no effect.

Ironically, in one telephone conversation shortly before our final eldership meetings, Pastor Phil queried me on how far we were prepared to go in restricting bizarre manifestations, qualifying this with, "You're going to get into developing a set of rules." How sad that he could not see he had already done so himself, by forbidding public discussion or pulpit sermons that would expose false doctrines and their purveyors.

Quite frankly, I grew very tired of the whole affair. Our charismatic legalism had robbed us of the freedom to seek actual truth. Every time we turned around, a new revelation steered us in another direction. My spiritual legs became heavy from running after every "wind of doctrine" that blew through our ranks. There was never a place of satisfaction, that Sabbath rest spoken of in Hebrews 4. While the anointing we pursued promised to be refreshing, all it did was hone, razor-sharp, the craving for another spiritual high. We at New Covenant were caught up on an unceasing merry-go-round.

But we are not so different from Old Testament Israel. They, too, ran after new and exciting ways of worship. They, too, thrilled at false signs and wonders, hung on the words of their multiplied false prophets, and substituted idols for the true God. But seeking the satisfaction they craved, they ran right past the only One who could offer it. The result was a maddening mix of gods that spiritually bled them dry.

Our Lord's remedy for them holds as true for us today. "Return, thou backsliding Israel and I will not cause mine anger to fall upon you, for I am merciful" (Jeremiah 3:12). We need to repent and return to Christ, who gives life and genuine refreshment:

> And Jesus said unto them, I am the bread of life: he that cometh to me shall never hunger; and he that believeth on me shall never thirst. (John 6:35)

A Rung Lower

Hope for change beat a hasty retreat after our second leadership meeting to discuss River teachings. Although loaded with Scriptures on false doctrine in the church, the written statement, prepared by Phil and handed out, did nothing to address specific problems in our congregation. The handout sheet became merely an irrelevant sideline, again pointing to "something somewhere out there," with scarcely a reference to the previous twelve years of damage done to our own people. Despite his exhortation that "The Lord and the apostles all agree that we are to examine all things, hold fast that which is good, and reject that which is erroneous," no admission of sin was forthcoming, nor public corrective measures taken.

Ironically, on my advice Phil had read the online version of the book authored by Ted Brooks, *I Was a Flakey Preacher*, and stated that he was looking at some of our doctrines in a different light. While I initially commended his remark, I was left dumbfounded in the face of his flood of contradictory statements. It became very apparent he had no real desire to initiate drastic, biblical change in our congregation.

The third and final meeting was nothing short of farcical. A brief handout was passed around, indicating Phil's stand on the manifestations prevalent in both our own and other River meetings. He preferred the middle of the road approach, and noted the possibility of God working through various types of manifestations. After noting that there were "lots of emotional responses to God's interaction with people in the Word," Phil went through the examples of the lame man healed in the Temple area, David dancing before the Ark of the Covenant, and Mary pouring the expensive ointment onto the head of Jesus. He concluded with "those who disparaged those responses were rebuked, and those who took offense suffered for it."

Phil's catalogue of examples is the classic comparison between apples and oranges. For him to suggest *any* similarity between Mary's anointing Jesus' head in worship, and the Toronto or Brownsville affairs with all their barking, roaring, dipping, crunching, birthing, screaming, drunkenness, etc., is to stretch credibility to the breaking point.

With a few minutes spent on the issues at hand, Phil announced with some satisfaction that we had all come to agreement, and it was time to move on. He then noted that this would be the end of discussing these issues in an eldership forum. Nor would we preach from the pulpit and publicly expose those within the movement whose prophecies had turned out false, who spoke contrary to very specific Scriptures, who pronounced anathema on dissenters … well, you get the idea. We would not even bother openly discussing the tide of false doctrine in which we had been immersed for the past dozen years— incredibly— for fear of causing "a weaker brother to stumble." The bottom line was that no one present saw the need to repent of anything.

And what about this so-called agreement we had all reached? We had agreed on absolutely nothing except that, since bizarre manifestations had happened to us, they were basically self-validating—that is, if that was the way we chose to believe. Amazingly, this was the general consensus. All present were free to believe just as we were convinced in our own hearts. If we chose to hold to a feeling that a confirmed false prophet was a true man of God in spite of it, then who was anyone to disagree?

The only concession was that New Covenant was not interested in promoting Toronto Blessing doctrine, and would not preach it before the congregation. But neither would they warn the congregation against it. It was a dead issue, as far as leadership was concerned, but Phil had no decisive answer to one disturbing question: "What are you going to do when someone again brings it into the congregation?"

It would not be long before he would have the opportunity to find out.

The rest of the meeting was a blur. For about an hour-and-a-half I just sat without speaking, looking away most of the time, stunned beyond words. While talk of upcoming church projects filled the remainder of the evening, I had already decided what needed doing. Further discussion was pointless. For a full year I had immersed myself in research and checked it meticulously against the Word of God. I was in possession of quotes, videotape, transcripts, cassette recordings, source material—you name it—and no one was interested enough to give it a second glance.

In the personal arena, I had lost sleep, fallen ill at times with the strain, been labeled, ridiculed, discredited, and had suffered through tremendous heartbreak and painful marital discord. And I came to realize there would be no repentance by the leadership at large in connection with anything we had done both congregationally and in our private devotional lives, despite what Scripture requires. It was time to begin the climb down from the ladder of super-spirituality. I'd had enough, and in that decision the peace of God filled my heart.

The next day I handed in my resignation letter from my eldership position and then sent a copy to every member of the leadership team. For the time being though, I continued to attend New Covenant Fellowship.

Playtime

Six weeks later, no one from the congregation had approached me, although at least a few had been told I no longer walked in the office of an overseer. The reality of it was, most had no idea this inquiry had been taking place the previous year. And they knew little or nothing of my research and discovery of the false teachings New Covenant was trafficking. The few who did know seemed to completely lack any understanding of why this was so urgent. And, sadly, no one was interested in viewing any of the research material on hand.

The first Sunday in December of 2000, Kris and I sat in our usual place in the front, along with Dale Lewis who helped lead worship and would give the message that day. He was one of those with whom Phil had spoken regarding my theological position, and he knew by then I had stepped down as elder. He was also aware that I was responsible for provoking the Toronto Blessing controversy in our congregation.

Just prior to the service that day, Kris and I had viewed a video by Iowa pastor Bill Randles titled *Fear Not, Little Flock*, in which Pastor Randles catalogued some of the latest River movement doctrines and contrasted them with Scripture. Kris had disagreed with some of his premise, and by the time we left for church, the presentation had caused some friction between us. In fact, things had been quite tense between us since my resignation, a tension that had been growing over the past year. Watching this video only seemed to make things worse.

When Dale took the pulpit, it didn't take five minutes until his purpose that day became crystal clear. I looked at Kris. Our eyes locked hard. This was it! Nice guy that he was, Dale had brought undiluted Toronto Blessing right back into our midst. Dale noted that while at first hesitant about the Toronto Blessing, he believed God told him to go and partake. He said he tried to talk God out of it, but the Lord persuaded him, saying that if the Azusa Street revival had been going on, Dale surely would have gone there. Succumbing, Dale went to Toronto and received prayer.

After his trip to Toronto to receive "the Blessing," Dale returned to his congregation. There he was prayed for (by his church's leadership), was slain in the spirit, and then, in his own words, "God came into the room." He said God dunked him three times with water and "played with him," taking him on the "water slides." Holy laughter resulted, and some time later he got up from the floor, wryly wondering where the theology was in that wild experience. Not that he doubted the vision's origin. He was fully convinced that God had done just what he related to all of us in the sanctuary that morning, and Dale had come to impart to us that same anointing.

Dale admitted to the congregation that he had no biblical reference point from which to judge his vision, but he maintained that it was evidence enough that his powerful experience was self-authenticating. It harkens back to the old Vineyard belief that if an experience produces good fruit, that in itself validates its holy origin. And based on an elastic definition of fruit, a person can claim to love Jesus more, yet easily discard scriptural prohibitions about altering His character. This reasoning was repeated for the last year of my tenure at New Covenant Fellowship—"It happened to me, so it was God."

Dale also downplayed head knowledge, a tired ploy used by so many in the River. Pitting the Word against the Holy Spirit is the easiest way in the world to get a Christian to believe that he is missing out. Since there are no reference points in Scripture from which to validate these manifestations, visions, dreams, and experiences, the best way to get around the issue is to declare the Bible relatively obsolete, or somehow detached from the Spirit's present leading. River participants deny doing this, but by their practice they affirm it is so.

It is a simple fact that right doctrine cannot be divorced from right practice. To admit to a whole new assembly line of manifestations and what-have-you because of eagerness to enter some new frontier of spirituality is to remove oneself from the only objective measuring rod in the church's possession. The apostle Paul repeatedly cautioned the church to cleave to sound doctrine.

Repeated glances at Kris during the service revealed plainly enough how heartbroken she was. She had believed in her leaders far longer than I, had defended them because she just knew they would come around to repentance. But it never happened. While Dale preached, and even invited the congregation forward to receive the impartation, Phil and Beth just sat in the front row of seats and watched. When we got up to leave abruptly at service's end, Beth turned to us as we walked past and nervously remarked that we should pick up one of the Christmas candles that had been decorated for each member. We declined and silently left the building.

How Much Are We Really Missing?

One of the main thrusts of this movement and its several tributaries of the Latter Rain, Dominion, and Word of Faith doctrines is the unfounded belief that the church has been missing out. We have been made to feel inadequate to the task, only half prepared for the Great Commission. And we have been made to think that what we need is something that only these super-spiritual teachers have to offer. I've met my share of them at New Covenant and have been tutored by some. I have myself, unfortunately, been prominent locally in other ways. How often in our cutting-edge services I felt superior to the ordinary Christian, as if I had some secret knowledge that would enable me to climb a bit higher onto some spiritual plane! It was only natural, since we were regularly told by our leadership that we had it. That in-crowd feeling was a natural high.

While this kind of thinking was downplayed some in the last couple years of Tom Smalley's pastorate, sermons preached in both the Sunday services and home meetings reinforced the belief that we were indeed riding the wave. We were on the edge of what God was doing, and we weren't about to return to the dry legalism of forbidding manifestations and doctrines that could not be found in the pages of Scripture.

That's the message of the super apostles, prophets, and teachers swarming the church in these last days. Listening to them is an exercise for the listener in humiliation when they tell us the church is asleep, naked, dead, or whatever, and they alone have what it takes to get her on the move once again. They prey on the desires of men to be more than they really are. It was this very craving in the Garden of Eden that prompted the first sin against God. Creating a hunger that cannot be satiated, these leaders prime the pump and pour the counterfeit wine. According to them, we've all got a black hole of theology that has sucked out real spiritual life, and we've been deficient for the past two thousand years, since the death of the last original apostles. But *they* can tell us how to get "it" back, unlock the secrets of spiritual success, and get in the flow of the Holy Spirit.

This whole mess is nothing more than neo-gnosticism, a free-for-all of spiritual secrets for the Christian gentry, a gradual progression for those initiates willing to forgo biblical caution and enter into the halls of knowledge reserved only for those who have an appropriate heart attitude. And money to burn.

Have Bucks, Will Travel

Scanning the itineraries recently of some of the new breed of apostles, prophets, and five-fold ministry preachers, it astonished me how much they traveled in a single year. Jetting not just across the North American continent, but to countries in the farthest reaches of the globe, these people convene gatherings in the Himalaya mountains to cast out the geographical demon known to them as the Queen of Heaven, tour the Ring Of Fire to impart their wisdom and manifestations at various churches, and fly to Australia to hold conferences while staying, of course, at plush resort hotels. It doesn't take a rocket scientist to figure out where all the green stuff is coming from. Check any of the big names in the prophetic field. Book after book, seminar after seminar, conference after conference. After book sales, conference and seminar fees are tabulated, if you're a prophet in the front running, then you've got a pretty good gross income. It's interesting that the true prophets of old and the original New Testament apostles didn't charge at all for the Gospel, but today's prophets, acting more *in the know* than even Paul or John, make a hefty living drawing in the crowds. As long as they're able to come up with one more hidden key to spiritual prosperity, as long as they can persuade the average believer that he is lacking in some Christian fundamental, today's gospel merchandisers will continue to draw the misinformed with their promises of more. And make them pay through the nose for it.

We have to come to grips with reality. As believers, we have never lacked anything that could give us a deep and satisfying walk with Christ. We have always, since the moment of our salvation, been complete in Him (Colossians 2:10). We have been made partakers of the divine nature through the magnificent promises of God (II Peter 1:3-4), and He is able to make all grace wonderfully abound toward us so that we have all sufficiency in every area of our lives (II Corinthians 9:8). We have the assurance of Scripture.

One of the major concessions Kris made just prior to our leaving New Covenant Fellowship was in the area of tithes. Our entire stay at this congregation was marked with a faithful giving of ten percent of all our gross income, regardless of how we were doing financially. While I would not leave New Covenant without Kris, I loathed giving any more of our hard-earned money to a group that for its entire existence had supported sundry false ministries. Without further hesitation, Kris and I agreed to stop giving our tithe to New Covenant and to disperse the monies to credible ministries and needy believers in our community.

I even began to question this whole issue of tithing. While all we ever heard preached was the cursing and blessing associated with Malachi 3:8-11, we never translated that into the New Testament realm. Whereas Old Testament tithing (giving ten percent) was mandatory, II Corinthians 9:7 tells us our giving is *not* to be compulsory but is rather to be done freely, as we each determine in our own hearts. The amount is left up to us, so long as we give willingly and cheerfully. We decide where our money goes, and how much, from a heart of love toward God.

Through enforced tithes and offerings, our church supported ministries that preached contrary to God's Word. By well-intentioned donations, we aided the worldwide propagation of a false gospel. By purchasing the books and videos of false prophets, by attending their seminars and running after their anointings, we put money in their pockets and enabled them to preach their version of Christ to an ever-widening congregation.

The River impartations and the movement's self-elevating view of wisdom haven't got a leg to stand on. In order to prosper, they require people to believe that God has somehow come up short in their lives, and that less privileged believers must travel to get "it," or buy the latest video or book installment, or attend the next conference for further instruction or power. The River teachers will not put it this way, of course, but that is exactly the implication, for if simple Christian folk are convinced that Christ is totally sufficient for them, they have no need to look elsewhere for a greater anointing.

The Cross was the greatest sacrifice and catalyst for the most fantastic gift in all creation, and nothing can be added to it. Its benefits inhabit every child of God who loves and serves his Lord, and who looks for Him to one day return in glory to take His own cherished loved ones home.

A Reluctant Goodbye

It took three days after the Toronto preaching of Dale Lewis to secure a meeting with Phil and Beth Clayton. In the interim, they did not attempt contact with us, though they must have known our reaction to Dale's presentation. When the appointed day arrived, we sat down opposite the couple in their living room and informed them as gently as possible, but point blank, that we needed to leave New Covenant Fellowship.

Phil immediately (and uncharacteristically) hardened, stating that he would not defend himself against what he no doubt perceived as accusations. In a soothing voice Beth asked to be given another chance, and asked if I would stay to teach them about the relevance of the material and the practical heresy in which we had been involved. She overlooked the glaring fact that I had already been attempting to do that very thing for more than a year, while being rebuffed at every level. Despite the hearings I was given, it was obviously never more than token appeasement. By the time of our last meeting, I had learned to discard any enticement that promised change. It simply wouldn't happen, and I knew it.

Kris tearfully explained her deep feelings of betrayal, at which point Beth interrupted her, saying there had been misunderstanding and they just needed more time. She noted that neither she nor Pastor Phil had known about the content of Dale Lewis' message. Both Kris and I countered with the argument that they could have called a halt to it at any time during the service. Phil quietly said that, upon Dale's mild protest of our congregation's seeming disinterest in receiving the Toronto impartation, he simply told Dale that he was comfortable with most of our membership's choice not to partake. I noted in response that Phil had not rebuked or attempted to correct Dale on the issue, but had let him lead the flock into an experience he fairly promised we'd never be confronted with. The bottom line was, he let Dale call the shots without so much as a murmur of disagreement.

Again with tears, Kris began pouring out her heart, speaking of the long patience with which we had carefully approached the subject matter for the entire past year, and the assurances we had received from New Covenant leadership that these issues were indeed being given consideration. Beth cut in to insert her own dialogue, at which Kris insisted she remain quiet long enough to hear what was being said in defense of our decision to leave.

When Kris finished, Beth continued with an unrealistic evaluation of the whole scenario. "When you come back…" she began.

At that, I jumped in with an incredulous, "Beth, we're not coming back!"

Taking a deep breath, she reiterated, "*When* you come back, we will receive you again." I could scarcely believe what I was hearing. She actually thought *we* would repent, and humbly return to the forgiveness of the fold.

When she sarcastically referred to my pulpit repentance during my sermon on Word of Faith errors, quite honestly, I lost it. I stood up in barely controlled anger and said to Kris, "We need to leave. Now!"

I had taken more than a year of verbal assault. I felt I could not accept it any longer.

Although I quickly phoned and apologized for losing my temper, and spoke to Phil a half-hour after the meeting, it was over—and we both knew it. Kris and I went home that day with a strangely empty feeling, empty because people with whom we had shared our lives for many years were going one way, while we were going another. While we had hoped it would not remain that way indefinitely, we also realized we do not always get what we hope for in this life.

CHAPTER 13

LiviNG ON THE OTHER SidE Of THE RivER

Five years have passed now since we left New Covenant Fellowship. Leaving this group of people we had come to know intimately and love was not easy. The adjustment for my family has been immense, mostly because our lives had been so centerd around the group. Suddenly we found ourselves swamped with free time. Kris, who for years had been pouring her artistic flair into the Sunday bulletins for New Covenant, was left with a huge and melancholy gap in her week. She considered this her personal ministry, and it was very satisfying. For her to sit before the computer without weekly printing to do was at first disheartening and a painful reminder of all the good times she had with people who were no longer a part of her life.

For me, although the joy of pursuing biblical integrity was exhilarating, it was sometimes offset by a feeling I can only describe in military terms. Like a soldier who had long wielded the sword and suddenly found himself in retirement, I felt very much alone. Having poured a year of my life into exposing fraudulence while attempting to turn the course of our beloved church group, I now found myself with nothing to do in a face-to-face context. In those night hours of that long mountain winter, I would stand in the darkness of my bedroom, staring out the window at the falling snow and asking myself, "Where are they? Does twelve years mean nothing?"

I reasoned that, even if the congregation thought we were wrong, surely they would seek us out in love and discuss the issues of our leaving. I had no such expectations of the leadership, but I was sure the rank and file membership, a fairly close group, would come and spend time with us, if for no other reason than to convince us of our wrong course of action or even just to hear our side of the story.

But only one person came. She stood outside our front door for a moment. It was one day before our first Christmas *outside*. She said she missed us, but she would not come into our house that day, nor did she ever come back again. Though we sent out a letter to New Covenant members detailing the false doctrine, no one telephoned us to discuss it. One New Covenant member did call to tell us that the leadership had given a vague and inaccurate explanation regarding our departure.

It took Tom Smalley a year-and-a-half to respond to my consistent emails to him. He noted that he was unable to think of anything to say ... a rather poor excuse considering my wife and I were his close friends for over a decade, and we had supported his ministry for his full pastorate. He finally agreed to read some of the evidence we had put together, but in the ensuing year-and-a-half he did not contact me.

My own family began meeting on Sunday afternoons with Bob and Jill Anderson, who had left New Covenant some months before we did. Together we explored the Scriptures without fear, ministered to one another, and sifted through all we had been through.

During this time, rumors spread that we had started our own church. This further exasperated us as we were just trying to pick up the pieces of our lives. Later we opened our home for occasional discernment meetings, which we advertised to the public. In these meetings, which still take place today, we examine doctrines both in our own lives and those rampant in the church. Here we offer a safe house for those wishing to look into the biblical justification (or lack of it) for such practices. Often those involved in River or similar groups undergo much the same kind of mind-numbing indoctrination as those in cults. False doctrine, hammered home repeatedly, erects walls to shut out the truth. Dismantling (i.e., deprogramming) such a fortification is often not easy. For people in these kinds of congregations, uniformity of belief is essential; therefore any dissenting voices are made to feel uncomfortable, if not blasphemous. *Prophecies* spoken over an individual confirming his relationship to the group, intense peer pressure to conform, or haranguing from the pulpit all have a dramatic effect on a person's ability to think for himself. Fear often keeps a dissatisfied church member in his place, and it can also plague him when he decides to leave. Exiting any harmful group can be very traumatic and is accompanied by an intense feeling of loneliness. So much time spent with a congregation in good times and bad has a profound effect on the human spirit. The temptation for some to return is so strong that they are willing to endure false teaching just to have some fellowship.

My family and I now quite happily attend an evangelical church and have been thrilled to be welcomed with open arms. The teaching is solid, biblical, and—think of it!—in context. We leave for home after each Sunday service feeling well fed spiritually and renewed by the fellowship.

Even though so much time has passed, I still marvel at how I fell for the enticements of some of the master manipulators of our day. Given a Christian twist, the foundations of elitism, religious sensuality, ingratiating personal prophecy, and false signs and wonders all made sense at the time, despite the inner promptings that consistently pointed me to the Scriptures that bade me examine everything *carefully*; hold fast to that which is good (I Thessalonians 5:21). Though saved, I watched and partook as the holy character of God was perverted, and our relationship to Him and the kingdom of God transformed into something that upon reflection chills me. I had believed that my leaders—the pastors, prophets, apostles, and sign-workers—knew better, and that the feelings of something terribly wrong in our congregation had to come from my own spiritual immaturity. My leaders told me so; therefore it was so.

Some would like to kid themselves into thinking that truth and biblical doctrine aren't so important, but they are. They are the detailed revelation of God our Creator Who loved us so much that He sent His Son, our Savior, to redeem us from the awful consequences of our sin by making atonement for us by His death on the Cross. Yes, doctrine is important enough for the apostle John to warn us, "Whosoever transgresseth, and abideth not in the doctrine of Christ, hath not God. He that abideth in the doctrine of Christ, he hath both the Father and the Son" (II John 9).

There definitely is mind control and spiritual manipulation taking place in much of Christendom today, not just in hyper-charismatic groups but in others as well. I was there, helped promote it, and spoke against those who rejected the latest *moves of God.* Following "every wind of doctrine," I drank deeply of every experience I could, followed our *prophets,* and preached with authority from an eldership position—until the day truth mattered.

History is filled with stories of those who have stood for truth, many of whom gave their lives to defend the faith God had put in their hearts. History is also filled with those who tried to squelch that truth. In his riveting account of the Nazi empire, historian William L. Shirer meticulously documents the internal workings of a system that once threatened to take over the world. *The Rise and Fall of the Third Reich* is a chilling account of the effects of mind-numbing propaganda.[1] The endless barrage of misinformation, incredibly, molded a once-beaten and fragmented people into the icon of elitism, which culminated in grisly death camps and the cold-blooded murder of those deemed lesser humans. A firsthand witness and opponent of the Nazi regime, Shirer recounted instances of conversation with German people, when he dared contradict the ludicrous governmental and media declarations of ethnic, cultural, and military superiority. He was met with shocked silence or an amazed stare. He noted that to question the Nazi machine's view of anything was considered blasphemy of the highest order. It dawned on him that the minds of many of the people had become so warped that they were no longer able to think for themselves or evaluate anything by a higher standard. Shirer observed that with the rise of the new German empire, the *truth* had become whatever Hitler and Goebbels said it was; they were the final arbiters of reality— spiritual and otherwise.

Some may think it is extreme to compare the spiritual deception and control tactics within the church today to that of the Nazi regime and the death camps, but we should remember that the church in Germany in the 1930s was very much like the church is today—having a head in the sand mentality about spiritual deception and turning religious leaders into super-human heroes who can do no wrong. Perhaps we are not all that different than Christians in Germany back then. We should not fool ourselves and think *we* would never be duped like that. The apostle Paul issued a warning to Christians:

> Now all these things happened unto them for ensamples: and they are written for our admonition, upon whom the ends of the world are come. Wherefore let him that thinketh he standeth take heed lest he fall. (I Corinthians 10:11,12)

Despite all of this, there is hope in the Lord; He is "Faithful and True" (Rev. 19:11). And He promised to preserve His church, that true body of believers whom He calls the Bride of Christ. Praise His name—there is hope. When truth is challenged, mocked, and thrown against the wind, we can be sure, it will never be altered. And that Word is a lamp unto our feet and a light unto our path.

The Lord is calling His people out from the midst of the false, to adhere to His truth, no matter what the cost. Let us respond with joy and thankfulness, knowing His grace is sufficient to strengthen us and give us courage.

> Let us go forth therefore unto him without the camp, bearing his reproach. For here have we no continuing city, but we seek one to come. (Hebrews 13:13-14)

ENdNotes

Why This Book

1. Dr. Herb Babcock, Former Member of Brownsville Assembly of God in his article "That's How They Do It In Toronto!" (http://www.deceptionin thechurch.com/prod03.html, accessed 01/07).

2. Stanley M. Burgess and Eduard M. van der Maas, *The New International Dictionary of Pentecostal and Charismatic Movements* (Grand Rapids, MI: Zondervan, 2002), p. 1149.

3. Mike Oppenheimer, "Tracing the Trail of the Revival" (Let Us Reason Ministries, http://www.letusreason.org/Pent30.htm, accessed 01/07).

Before the Beginning

1. Gwen R. Shaw, *Redeeming the Land* (Jasper, AR: Engeltal Press, 1987).

2. Ibid., pp. 107-113.

3. Gwen R. Shaw, *Our Ministering Angels* (Engeltal Press, 1986).

4. Ibid., p. 52.

5. Ibid., p. 6.

6. Ibid., p. 117.

7. Ibid., p. 136.

8. Ibid., pp. 69-70.

9. Rick Joyner, *The Final Quest* (New Kensington, PA: Whitaker House, 1996).

1/The Emergence of the God-Men

1. The teachings of Kenneth Copeland and Kenneth Hagin (such as the ones mentioned in chapter one) are documented in many different articles and books. The following articles list many quotes (and their actual sources) by Copeland and Hagin that substantiate their views: "Maturity Training" by Sandy Simpson (http://www. deceptioninthechurch.com/maturitytraining.html, "Hagin Drunk 'in the Spirit'" by David W. Cloud (http://wayoflife.org/fbns/hagindrunk.htm) and "Return of the God/Men by Mike Oppenheimer (http://www. letusreason.org/Wf17.htm). For a list of books that document the teachings of Copeland, Hagin, and other's of the same spiritual proclivities, see Resources for Further Information at the back of this book.

2. Mike Oppenheimer, "The Manifest Sons of God" (http://www. let usreason.org/Latrain1.htm, accessed 01/07).

3. Citing the Bible Page, "John Avanzini" (http://www. thebiblepage.org /avoid/avanzini.shtml, accessed 01/07).

4. Mike Oppenheimer, "Death by Faith" (http://www. letus reason. org/Wf25.htm, accessed 1/2007).

5. D.R. McConnell, *A Different Gospel* (Peabody, MA: Hendrickson Publishers, 1988).

6. Larry Parker and Don Tanner, *We Let Our Son Die* (Eugene, OR: Harvest House Publishers, 1980).

3/The Prince of Persia

1. Larry Lea, *Could You Not Tarry One Hour* video series (Okemos, MI: Harbinger International).

2. Identificational Repentance: The act of confessing before God the sins of, and identifying with the guilt of, your country, people group (ethnicity), and ancestors, and asking forgiveness to break a curse on the land. Reconciliation Walk: Basically a march in which Christians join with Muslims, Jews, Blacks, or anyone we figure was hurt by us in some point in history, to accomplish healing between races and opposing religions.

3. "March for Jesus" started in 1987 in London, UK, and eventually became known as "Global March for Jesus." "March for Jesus, USA" began in 1989.

4. C. Peter Wagner is president of Global Harvest Ministries and Chancellor of the Wagner Leadership Institute. He is considered a major figure in the church growth movement.

4/We All Fall Down

1. Kenneth Hagin conference video/DVD, "Kenneth Hagin and the Spirit of the Serpent" by Joseph E. Chambers (Charlotte, NC: Paw Creek Ministries). To order this dvd, 800/338-7884.

2. Ted Brooks, *I Was a Flakey Preacher* (Westlock, AL, Canada: Guardian Books, 1999).

3. G. Richard Fisher with M. Kurt Goedelman, "Benny Hinn's Move into Necromancy" citing Benny Hinn sermon, *Double Portion Anointing*, Part #3, Orlando Christian Center, Orlando, Fla., April 7, 1991. From the series, *Holy Ghost Invasion*.

4. Mike Oppenheimer citing Rodney Howard-Brown, "The New Anointing" (Let Us Reason ministries, http://www.letusreason.org/Pent40.htm, accessed 01/07).

5. "New Year 1998 - Where To Now?" article by Christian Witness Ministries (Australia) citing Wes Campbell's Braveheart speech. (http://www.christian-witness.org/archives/cetf1998/newyear 1998.html, accessed 01/07).

6. Carol Arnott speaking at the Arise Deborah women's conference in Pensacola, Florida, January 1999, documented by Jewel Grewe, "The Sea of Subjectivity" (Discernment Ministries newsletter, March/April 1999, Volume #2, Issue #10, http://www.discernment-ministries.org/1999_March April.pdf, accessed 01/07).

5/The Word of the Lord?

1. John Hinkle prophecy June 9, 1994 (See the Berean Call's Question and Answer at: http://www.thebereancall.org/Newsletter/questionanswer/1993/dec93b.php).

2. Rick Joyner, *The Final Quest*, op. cit., pp. 89-90.

3. Dave Hunt, T. A. McMahon, *The Seduction of Christianity* (Eugene, OR: Harvest House Publishers, 1985).

6/Every Wind of Doctrine

1. Keith Intrater, *Covenant Relationships* (Shippensburg, PA: Destiny Image Publishers, 1989).

2. Roland Buck, *Angels On Assignment* (New Kensington, PA: Whitaker House, 1979).

3. Rick Joyner, *The Final Quest* , op. cit., p. 90.

4. Ibid., pp.20-21, 28.

5. Rev. Ron Stringfellow, "Latter Day Deception" (Deception in the Church e-newsletter, January 1998 at http://www.deceptioninthechurch.com /ditc11.htm, accessed 01/07).

6. David W. Cloud, "Hagin Drunk 'in the Spirit'" (Fundamental Baptist Information Service, October 4, 1998, http://www.wayoflife.org/fbns/hagindrunk.htm, accessed 01/07).

7. Bruce Thompson, *The Divine Plumbline* (Colorado Springs, CO: Crown Ministries, International, 1984).

8. Carl Widrig Jr., "The PK Fax Scandal Re James Ryle's Comments on the Beatles" (http://www.geocities.com/hebrews928/beatles.html, accessed 01/07).

9. Albert James Dager, *Vengeance Is Ours* (Sword Publishers, 1990), p. 226.

10. For information on the beliefs of Randy Shankle, read "Kingdom Theology" by Albert James Dager (posted at Eastern Regional Watch Ministries, http://www.erwm.com/KingdomTheology2.htm, accessed 01/07).

11. Benny Hinn, *Good Morning Holy Spirit* (Nashville, TN: Thomas Nelson Publishers, 1990), p. 135.

12. "The Spirit of Truth and the Spirit of Error," op. cit.: For detailed documentation on the ministry of Benny Hinn, visit http://www.christianresearch service.com (Christian Research Service).

13. Rodney Howard-Brown, *The Touch of God* (Tulsa, OK: Albury Publishing, 1998), pp. 13-14.

14. For more information on Sam Fife and the Manifest Sons of God, read *Joel's Army* by Jewel Grewe (Discernment Ministries, 1991, 2nd edition 2006, http://www.discernment-ministries.org/JoelsArmy1.htm, accessed 01/07).

Chapter 7

1. A term used by Charles and Francis Hunter in their book, *Holy Laughter* (Kingwood, TX: Hunter Books, 1994), pp. 5-7.

2. Warren Smith, "Holy Laughter or Strong Delusion?" (Discernment Ministries, http://www.discernment-ministries.org/Holy_Laughter.htm, accessed 01/07).

3. Ibid.

4. Ibid.

5. A six minute video clip of a "holy laughter" meeting with Kenneth Copeland and Kenneth Hagin can be viewed at http://www.youtube.com/watch?v=AjujnAs-6tM.

Chapter 8

1. Ray Yungen, *A Time of Departing* (Silverton, OR: Lighthouse Trails Publishing, 2nd edition, 2006), p. 34.

2. "Highlights in the Life of William Marrion Branham" (The Bible Believers Association, Inc., http://www.biblebelievers.org/bblife.htm, accessed 1/07).

3. In 1980, Oral Roberts claimed to have seen a 900-foot-tall Jesus.

4. Rick Joyner, *The Final Quest*, op. cit., p. 11.

5. In 1978, cult leader Jim Jones lead over 900 followers in a mass suicide in northern Guyana.

6. Mary Owen "Oregon Church Says Gold Dust, Feathers Fell During Meetings" (*Charisma* magazine, September 2000, http://www.charisma mag.com/display.php?id=517, accessed 01/07).

Chapter 9

1. Bill Randles, *Weighed and Found Wanting* (Cambridge, Great Britain, 2nd ed., 1996), p. 179, citing Rick Joyner, "The Unfolding of a Prophet," (*Fullness*, Jan/Feb 1990), p. 13.

2. Benny Hinn crusade in Denver, Colorado in September 1999 (listen to video clips at http://www.intotruth.org/wof/Hinn.html, accessed 01/07).

3. C. Peter Wagner, *Acts of the Holy Spirit* (Ventura, CA: Regal Books/ Gospel Light, 2000),   pp. 51, 123.

4. See http://www.bible.ca/tongues-audio-video-documentation.htm for audio/video clips of various leaders including clips on "drinking houses" and "drinking songs."

Chapter 10

1. *Arise Deborah* conference with Carol Arnott, op. cit.

2. John Wimber: 1934-1997. Wimber's "paradigm shift" is discussed and documented in several books and articles such as C. Peter Wagner's *Acts of the Holy Spirit* (Ventura, CA: Regal Books, 2000), p. 123.

3. Brian Flynn, *Running Against the Wind* (Silverton, OR: Lighthouse Trails Publishing, 2nd edition, 2005), pp. 164-165.

4. John Goodwin, "Testing the Fruit of the Vineyard" (quoting John Wimber from the Vineyard '83, Leadership Conference, "The Five Year Plan," http://www.biblebelievers.net/Charismatic/kjcviney.htm, accessed 01/07).

5. Anges Sanford, *The Healing Light* (New York, NY: Ballantine Books, Ballantine Edition, 1983).

6. Morton Kelsey, *Healing and Christianity* (New York, NY: Harper and Row, 1973), p. 51.

7. Ibid., p. 332.

8. Ibid., p. 338.

9. John Goodwin, "Testing the Fruit of the Vineyard," op. cit.

10. Franklin Hall, *Atomic Power with God Through Fasting and Prayer,* 1946.

11. Albert James Dager, *Vengeance is Ours* (Redmond, WA: Sword Publishers, 1990). p. 51.

12. Mary Owen, "Oregon church says gold dust, feathers fell during meetings" (*Charisma* magazine, September 2000, http://www. charisma mag.com / display.php?id=517, accessed 02/07); also see "There's Gold in Them Thar Teeth" by Mike Oppenheimer, http://www.letusreason.org/Pent5.htm, accessed 02/07.

13. Mike Oppenheimer, "The Teachings of 'the Prophet' William Branham" (Let Us Reason ministries, http://www.letusreason.org/Latrain4.htm, accessed on 01/07).

14. Ibid. For photos, history and detailed information on William Branham, see http://www.biblebelievers.org.

15. For a timeline and information on Sandford, see History and Times of the Kingdom (http://www.fwselijah.com/timeline.htm, accessed 01/07).

16. Nathan C. Miller, "The Kingdom Incorporated - Truth or Error" (History and Times of the Kingdom, http://www.fwselijah.com/nathan .htm, accessed 01/07).

17. Sarah E. Parham, *The Life of Charles F. Parham: Founder of the Apostolic Faith Movement;* (New York, NY: Garland Publishing, Inc., 1930, 1985), p. 32, figure 6 (photo); also see: http://www.seekgod.ca/father parham.htm, accessed 02/07.

18. R. J. Smith, *The Great Black Way: L.A. in the 1940s and the Lost African-American Renaissance* (New York, NY: Perseus Books Group: Public Affairs Books, 2006), p. 168.

Chapter 11

1. David Wilkerson, "The Reproach of the Solemn Assembly" (Times Square Church, 1999, http://www.webedelic.com/church/sacred.htm, accessed 01/07).

Chapter 13

1. William L. Shirer, *The Rise and Fall of the Third Reich* (New York, NY: Simon and Schuster/Touchstone, 1959).

Index

A

A Different Gospel 37
Alpha Course 13
Ananias and Sapphira 21, 194
Angels On Assignment 107
animal sounds 87, 168, 183, 196, 197
anointing 13, 22, 29, 56, 57, 64, 69, 73, 78, 79, 80, 82, 93, 94,
        95, 110, 115, 117, 118, 121, 128, 129, 131, 132, 133, 135,
        136, 156, 160, 165, 174, 175, 180, 190, 197, 200, 202, 205,
        208
apostle Paul 18, 51, 52, 53, 56, 66, 67, 90, 94, 139, 151, 167,
170, 187, 198, 205, 207
Arnott, Carol 80
Arnott, John 13
Assemblies of God 110, 171, 191
Atomic Power with God Through Fasting and Prayer 172, 173
Avanzini, John 35
Azusa Street Revival 177, 179, 204

B

barking 202
Beatles, the 117
Bickle, Mike 187
Branham, William 147, 172, 173, 174
Brooks, Pastor Ted 76, 201
Brownsville Revival 13, 21, 22, 83, 156, 179, 202
Buck, Roland 107

C

Catholicism 16, 192, 199, 200
Charisma magazine 36, 162, 182, 221
Clark, Randy 12
cleansing 44, 86, 87
Coe, Jack 36
Copeland, Kenneth 14, 27, 36, 37, 41, 42, 81, 103, 109, 113,

out of alignment 40

P

paradigm shift 166, 179
Parham, Charles Fox 177, 178
Pensacola Outpouring 22, 81, 156
Pentecostalism 4, 13, 20, 26, 131, 144, 146, 177, 183
positive confession 27, 33, 34, 35, 42, 169
prayer walking 65
prophecy 21, 26, 39, 82, 85, 86, 87, 88, 90, 92, 93, 94, 95, 96,
        97, 98, 99, 101, 102, 110, 111, 113, 143, 146, 162, 172, 213
prophetic movement 91, 97, 147, 187
prophets 20, 22, 88, 89, 90, 91, 92, 93, 95, 96, 99, 112, 118, 119, 137,
        147, 148, 149, 151, 170, 172, 175, 176, 178, 180, 194, 201,
        206, 207, 208, 213, 214

R

Randles, Pastor Bill 204
rapture, the 113, 127, 158, 170, 171, 175, 177
reconciliation walks 63
Redeeming the Land 16, 17, 62, 217
revelation knowledge 50, 149, 175
River movement 12, 13, 82, 95, 116, 152, 162, 168, 169, 188,
        191, 196, 201, 204, 205
Roberts, Oral 36, 101, 148

S

Sandford, Frank W. 177, 178
Sanford, Agnes 169
Shaw, Gwen R. 16, 17
shotgun prophecy 97
sickness 30, 35, 36, 37, 38, 39, 41, 42, 43, 46, 113, 177
signs and wonders 24, 39, 76, 92, 131, 171, 177, 201, 213
slain in the spirit 39, 73, 75, 76, 77, 78, 80, 109, 130, 134, 136,
        157, 185, 189, 196
Smith, Warren 138
soul ties 108
spiritual drunkenness 40, 128, 129, 136, 162, 179, 196, 202
spiritual mapping 61, 62, 67

Resources for Further Information

Books

I Was a Flakey Preacher by Pastor Ted Brooks
ISBN 1894169794, Guardian Books

The Seduction of Christianity by Dave Hunt
ISBN 0890814414, Harvest House Publishers

Vengeance is Ours by Albert James Dager
ISBN 0962663204, Sword Publishers

Weighed and Found Wanting by Bill Randles
ISBN 0964662612, St. Matthew Publications
Online edition: http://www.believersingrace.com/images/WFW1.PDF

Websites

Christian Research Service: www.christianresearchservice.com
Christian Witness Ministries: www.christian-witness.org
Deception in the Church: www.deceptioninthechurch.com
Discernment Ministries: www.discernment-ministries.com
Eastern Regional Watch Ministries: www.erwm.com
Kjos Ministries: www.crossroad.to
Let Us Reason Ministries: www.letusreason.org

Other Books by Lighthouse Trails Publishing

Another Jesus
by Roger Oakland
$12.95, ISBN: 978-0-9791315-2-3, Fall 2007

A Time of Departing, 2nd Ed.
by Ray Yungen
$12.95, ISBN: 978-0-9721512-7-6

Faith Undone
by Roger Oakland
$12.95, ISBN: 978-0-9791315-1-6

For Many Shall Come in My Name, Revised 2nd Ed.
by Ray Yungen
$12.95, ISBN: 978-0-9721512-9-0

Laughter Calls Me, 2nd Ed.
by Catherine Brown
$12.95, ISBN: 978-0-9721512-6-9

Running Against the Wind, 2nd Ed.
by Brian Flynn
$12.95, ISBN: 0-9721512-5-7

Tapestry: The Journey of Laurel Lee
by Laurel Lee (author of *Walking Through the Fire*)
$15.95, ISBN: 0-9721512-3-0

Trapped in Hitler's Hell
by Anita Dittman with Jan Markell
$12.95, ISBN: 978-0-9721512-8-3

To Order Additional Copies of:

The Other Side of the River

send $12.95 plus $3.75 (for 1 book) to:
Lighthouse Trails Publishing
P.O. Box 958
Silverton, Oregon 97381

Call or go online for information about quantity discounts.

You may order online at
www.lighthousetrails.com
or
Call our toll-free number:
866/876-3910
[ORDER LINE]

For all other calls: 503/873-9092
Fax: 503/873-3879

The Other Side of the River, as well as all books by Lighthouse
Trails Publishing, can be ordered through all major outlet stores,
bookstores, online bookstores and Christian bookstores.

Bookstores may order through
Ingram, Spring Arbor, or Send the Light.
Libraries may order through Baker and Taylor.

Quantity discounts available for most of our books.
International orders may be placed either online, through e-mail or
by faxing or mailing order form.

For more information:
Lighthouse Trails Research Project
www.lighthousetrailsresearch.com
or visit the author's website at:
www.theothersideoftheriver.com